TO John,

WHAT A DELIGHT TO SEE YOU
AGAIN AFTER ALL THESE YEARS —
WHILE OUR " HOUSES " HAVE AGED
A BIT — I STILL FEEL THE
SAME SPIRIT OF OUR
YOUTH

life in small bites

moments in time…

WARMEST REGARDS

TED DREISINGER

TED

DEDICATION

For Molly, who for some unknown reason asked me to marry her, and for more than three decades has been my partner, confidant and friend.

To my sister Nancy, who for the 62 years of her all too short life shined, and with unquenchable passion lifted the lives of all those who were privileged to know her.

TABLE OF CONTENTS

A TURNING OF THE PAGE...4

MIRROR, MIRROR ON THE WALL.......................................8

MOMENTS IN TIME...11

BE AND NOT SEEM...14

THE BEAT GOES ON...17

SOMETIMES YOU JUST HAVE TO WALK AWAY...................21

IT'S ABOUT THE BREATH..24

TEACHING OLD DOGS..26

HOW ABOUT THOSE HANDS...31

THE CLOCK IS TICKING..35

SUBWAYS IN BERLIN...39

DOWNS - NOT OUT..42

CANADIAN SUMMERS...47

JUST A GAME..52

LIFE AND THE DESERT...58

SPEED MAY NOT KILL, BUT CAN TEACH........................62

RUGBY, SCHOOL KIDS, MEANING.................................66

EVERY OTHER BOOK..70

COMING HOME...74

THREE CATS AND THE SETTING SUN.............................78

LISTEN TO THIS...82

PASSING THE BATON..85

EVERY DAY BEGINS AGAIN..89

DOORS AND STORES..92

IT'S GOOD TO COME HOME...96

THINGS WE FIND AT 40,000 FEET 100

TWO STORIES MAKE ONE 105

RANDOM ACTS...110

THE STRING NO LONGER VIBRATES 114

SOMEBODY TOUCHED ME...118

IT ONLY TAKES A MOMENT..121

CHILDREN PLAY..125

THE PHANTOM FIVE...128

IT'S HARDLY EVER WHAT YOU THINK 132

COFFEE AND CAMELS...136

WORDS CAN HURT, BUT... 141

SOMEONE WAS AT THE DOOR...145

KIDS...YOU'VE GOT TO LOVE THEM...149

MENU PLEASE...153

GRAVITY, NOT JUST A GOOD IDEA...IT'S THE LAW 156

IT'S IN THE REARVIEW MIRROR...159

ACKNOWLEDGMENTS

This book would not have been possible without a number of people. My parents, of course, set the 'lens' of perception through which I have spent my life. To my sister Anne, for her brilliant talent and example of unrelenting kindness.

Harold 'Deacon' Duval and Walden Skinner, a coach and academic respectively who set unrelenting examples of "...yes you can..." on the horizons of my young life. Garth Russell, an orthopedist, who by simply performing the calling set before him, brought me along, mentored and changed the course of my life forever. Vert Mooney, a brilliant orthopedist and richly coveted friend who taught me more about navigating professional minefields than anyone I have ever known. Scott Leggett, who found himself in the cross-hairs of Vert's mind and skill. His friendship, personal and professional, have been without measure. Arthur Jones, inventor of Nautilus and MedX, whose creative genius befriended and permitted me a career, with things to say. Robin McKenzie, a New Zealand physiotherapist/entrepreneur whose equal genius and friendship opened doors through which I have had some of the richest experiences of my life.

To Bob Smith entrepreneur, gentle soul, who through a chance meeting as seatmates in the exit row of an airplane, became a friend and encouraged me to continue writing just when I needed to hear it...sage advice I thankfully followed. To Paul Flicker and Monica Schultz, dear and loving friends who poked and prodded me to be more assertive, without whose loving and pragmatic support, these latter years would have been less fun.

To Alexis Powers, a smart driven woman and director of a writer's workshop in Tucson, who was unrelenting in her encouragement to"...get that book published!!!"

To Jenifer Doherty (www.jeniferdoherty.com), whose keen eye and mind designed the cover helping me understand that sometimes less is more.

Finally, to Harry G. 'Jim' Priester, coach and academic who knew more about how to motivate and energize young men than anyone I ever met. I was fortunate to find myself in the bulls-eye of this gifted man early in my life. His influence continues to this day.

INTRODUCTION

We all have stories to tell. People we have known, places we have visited, the strange and curious ways our lives have been changed by what appeared to be the smallest of events.

It seems that every time you think you have seen it all, something happens to make it clear there is a lot more out there to see.

This book is a collection of observations and reflections made over several years of writing a weekly blog – deadlined Sunday mornings. There is no particular theme in the text; they are not connected by a particular thread or story line, but simply musings that help my appreciation for the richness of life and how they have helped me understand how little I really know, and a little more about the journey we all experience.

If there is any continuity at all it is the first and last entry. The book begins with the loss of my sister to early onset Alzheimer's and ends with the unwavering faith that she lives on…

A TURNING OF THE PAGE

"For this corruptible must put on incorruption,
and this mortal *must* put on immortality. So when this
corruptible shall have put on incorruption, and this mortal
shall have put on immortality, then shall be brought to pass the
saying that is written, Death is swallowed up in victory."
1 Corinthians 15:53, 54 - Bible

Her head was tilted back and to the right…eyes closed….mouth agape.

Breath in…breath out…breath in…breath out...

The breaths were shallow and while coming fairly regularly, they were clearly not normal. It was a hollow almost mechanical sound; a sound that if it were dark and one were alone, it might be unnerving…indeed it 'was' unnerving.

Her first breath, as for all of us, had been a deep gasp – from darkness to light…fighting for a new life…a birth…an open check book…a tabula rasa – everything in front of her…pages to be turned…experiences yet to find their way to the novel that would become her life…all in front of her with nothing but blue sky!

It is not that way for these breaths – breath in….breath out….breath in….breath out. No, these breaths were increasingly shallower by the smallest of increments and they signaled the other end of the journey…the 'end' of the journey...

Back to Missouri…

It was getting to be the end of the whale-watching season, and I had a friend visiting from the East. I thought a mid-morning kayaking adventure might be fun. The tour had been planned for several weeks, and after missing the whales the last time out, there was hope of success this time. The day before a Grey Whale had breached a couple of miles from shore…would it happen again?

The phone was in the car…the calls came, but there was no one to answer. When we finished the 'whale-less' watching event, we headed back to the shop, changed from wet suits to our street clothes and headed for the car…the car and my phone.

There were six text messages and three calls on the 'you missed me' list. It was pretty clear something was terribly wrong. Dark thunderclouds were gathering on the horizon of that sunny Southern California sky.

Nancy had aspirated some liquid. This led to a compromise in her breathing a reduction in her blood oxygen levels…not a good sign. Rushed to the hospital, she was stabilized, but it was clear the end was near. She had 'do not resuscitate' wishes, as do all in our family…not wanting extraordinary medical interventions taking place when the quality of our lives no longer had meaning.

"When can you be here?"

The question was both matter of fact and urgent. Mariah related the doctor's opinion that her mother might not last the night. It was all happening too fast…fast, but with clarity. "I'll be out first thing in the morning, in St. Louis by 5:30 and the hospital by 8PM," I replied. "She might not make it." Mariah said, but it was the best that could be done.

I called my other sister in Virginia, made flight reservations, ate a quiet dinner and headed for bed. Of little doubt, the next day would be long. Anne met me in St. Louis and we made the, by now all too familiar, drive together to Columbia.

It was not good…

We arrived to a varied group of people both at the door and in the room my sister occupied. A number of Mariah's classmates had set vigil with her, as well as folk from Nancy's former church – some older and some that had grown up around her from their childhood. She had a way with children…she had a way with everyone!

Anne asked to spend a few minutes of private time with Nancy. When she was finished, I slipped in to hold her in my arms, to thank her for the life she had given to me, to say how proud I was to have been her brother, and wondered out loud if the decisions I had made had been the best…I asked forgiveness if they had not.

After most of the folk left, Mariah, Anne and I were alone in the room with Nancy. We chatted quietly as Mariah gently put eye drops into her mother's eyes, some moisturizer around her nose, and softly swabbed her mouth…all the while kissing her, speaking to her, touching her, stroking her and ministering in the most sacred of ways known only to a daughter and best friend. We talked to Nancy letting her know it was okay to let go…it was time…it was right…it was safe.

Mariah had been up for three days, by now and needed some sleep. Before tucking into a chair across the hall for a few hours, she slipped into bed with her mother and snuggled close as they had done so often in their lives. Her head resting on Nancy's shoulder and hand on her chest…the tenderness of this act exquisite.

The breathing more ragged now…...breath in…...breath out……breath in…….breath out……

Anne and I stayed up…kept the watch – she reclined on a chair by the bed and I sat in front of my keyboard trying to understand the fearfulness and serenity of the moment. I was watching my sister die, and in the most ironic of ways…in ways words fail to express…it was the most loving and intimate experience I ever had with her.

Breath in…………breath out…………breath in…………breath out………..

6

She slipped quietly away from us this afternoon, and I was reminded of these words, "…into thy hands I commend my spirit…"

Breath out………..

MIRROR, MIRROR ON THE WALL

The electric shaver hummed as I moved it to the left side of my face, when I glanced up and first noticed.

In fact it was a bit startling, not just because it was so apparent, but also because it had eluded me, unseen for so long – my whole life in fact. There is no other way to say this, but this morning when I looked in the mirror, my father was staring back at me!

My dad!! What the heck was he doing there?!

In that moment, it seemed odd that I hadn't seen it before. I mean, in reality I have performed this ritual thousands of times. Maybe I hadn't taken notice, because shaving is one of those oft repeated, thoughtless habits one performs…you know, routine activities – wandering minds.

Little doubt, however, for those brief moments, 'he' had my attention.

This event brought to mind what I have heard said for decades by folk in their golden… thoughtful… mature …senior…less relevant…hmmm, I know, "we have survived and are still on the planet" years – yeah, that's it!

You have heard it too:

"When I looked in the mirror today, I wondered who that old man/woman was staring back at me. I know I'm _____ (fill in the blank), but I don't feel like I'm that old!"

Not much thought given…

I am not often reminded the years are slipping by with the increasing velocity of a brakeless, runaway freight train, maybe because there is still plenty to occupy my mind…places to go…people to see, OR maybe because - if there is nothing to do - I make an effort to manufacture projects to occupy my time.

This morning there was none of that, and for the briefest of moments I saw my father as a 67-year-old man…a tired looking 67-year-old man…staring at me with equal curiosity.

Older people I know, talk about the depressingly unrelenting markers in their lives. Decade birthdays are a common example:

"Man," they say, "I just turned 30. My life is over!" or

"People tell me, life begins at 40, but it seems to me this is a long way from a beginning!"

For me, those decade markers slipped by like any other day – no feelings of passing milestones…no moments of reflective melancholy…no sense that youth or middle age were gone forever.

Nope! If anything reminds me that time has slipped by it might be an old high school classmate telling me they are grandparents, or by now great grandparents! There are a few others that have drawn my attention to the current period I occupy in life's expedition – but not many.

The thing is - the 'I' – the little creature/soul/life energy who lives inside of me doesn't feel any age at all…I simply am! If I were to try and express it, as I look out the windows of the 'organic mud house' in which I live, I do not feel any different now than I did when I was 5 or 10 or 40 or 60!

Of course, my body is older…it's batteries slowly running down in spite of a daily – or rather nightly – recharge. Regardless of all the rejuvenating activity that occurs when we sleep, it seems that even the best 'genetic rechargeables,' imperceptibly reduce their capacity to fully refill, and over time physical capacity diminishes.

It is also true that I have learned a lot more stuff since I was a youngster, and little doubt the things I have put in my mind influence the things that I do, or do not do.

BUT in the context of life in this world, I truly see myself as a timeless passenger sitting in the control room of a piece of living protoplasm identified as 'Ted,' pushing buttons, pulling levers and filling the hard drives with information that provides my 'space suit' nourishment, protection from the elements and built in routines, many of which run on automatic pilot (e.g. breathing, heartbeat, digestion, injury repair, disease destruction, among so many others), permitting 'me' to focus on other things…you know like shaving!

Seeing my 'father' in the mirror was startling, because regardless of the unrelenting effects of time and gravity, I still face life with the same optimism and excitement I always have. Maybe the 'garment' I have worn for so many decades is dog-eared and a little thin around the edges…BUT a garment nonetheless – nothing more than the address where I have spent my life.

It won't be too awfully long now, when I will be looking for a new residence…a fresh place to live…a home where I can peek out through a another set of windows to see what lies just outside…a place where I will fill the hard drives with new and interesting information.

I wonder if there will be mirrors?

MOMENTS IN TIME

There are those moments…
"The happiest man is he who learns
from nature the lesson of worship."
- Emerson RW; <u>Nature</u>

The skies above the Western slope of the Catalina Mountains were the kind of vision only a creative artist could paint. The high nimbostratus clouds darkened, knitting together a living black and white shaded patchwork quilt with an intricacy that was at the same time intimate and overwhelming.

Lower, lightly colored cumulus clouds sat under the covering blanket in just the right places; accented in pinks and salmon. It was a visual paradox to see the lightly colored cotton balls capture the setting sun to the west – a dynamic and living tapestry, shifting every few seconds…changing with a compelling magnetic draw that dared you to look away…dared you to miss the subtle shift on the living canvas lasting but a few minutes – never to be seen again by anyone…anywhere…at anytime. It was awesome!

The wind at ground level was strong. The kind of wind, that blowing through tree leaves carries with it a rustling sound undulating in and out with a hypnotic and unpredictable rhythm…equally compelling to the rapidly darkened sky – the shift from visual to auditory predominance so smooth, so subtle, that as your mind yielded to this symphony, the rich, dark tones drew you into its creative force...life giving, familiar, fully integrated.

A little context…

My early life, meaning all of my early life, there was a part of the year to which I looked forward without variance and without fail. My mother's people had some land on a beautiful lake in a magical region of Central Ontario, Canada called Muskoka. It was the Camelot of my youth. We had a cottage on the shores of Lake Joseph where we spent the month of August every year through my mid to late twenties.

In my early years, a number of relatives shared a 'family cottage' at different times during the summer, but as the years passed and families grew, each spread out and built little places near the water's edge of Stanley bay. There are so many things that could be said…so many people who I loved and in return loved me…so many experiences recorded in the nether regions of my mind, accumulated from decades during those days in the month of August when we disappeared from life and slipped into hardwood forests of maple and pine of our"…never never land…"

The old family cottage had a covered veranda with sections of vertical pine logs supporting the overhanging roof and a lovely railing made up of smaller pine pieces with even smaller branches crisscrossing and attached to the its horizontal base. It was about 20 feet long and 8 feet or so deep, and a favorite place for me to sit during rainstorms as the summer skies brought occasional rainy days with thunderous lightening snapping bright for milliseconds and bringing a sense of oneness to my soul.

Sometimes gusty winds would blow the rain onto the porch driving most of us indoors. But for me, there was a secret place on that old veranda - a screened in bunk bed recessed on the far end by the broad stairs at the head of a path leading to the boathouse. When the rains came and strong winds blew, I would slip into the bottom bunk and drift into a magical timeless place where I felt fully alive.

My mother had taught us to love and respect nature. Water was deadly, but if carefully respected a "…gift from God." Storms could be dangerous, but their sights and sound were "…reminders of just how awesome our Creator is." Like Pavlov's dog, when the storms came, because of her love and the safety we felt in her presence, we embraced their power and relished in the astounding strength they represented. To this day, when the storms come, the strength and love my mother planted so long ago, returns to fill my soul with excitement and anticipation.

The here and now...

Tonight, as the desert monsoon storm approached, I found myself returning to the land of my birth and the screened in porch that was, for me an almost sacred place. Tonight as the winds picked up and the rains came I moved inside behind the screen door in my little home office. I lay back in the chair with my feet up as Leah slipped in and lay on the mat by the door purring at my feet. She felt the calm that had been planted in me so long ago and joined in a timeless moment of bliss.

When I returned to my little office from the 'place' I had found with Leah, the winds and thunderous rain, I had been drifting for a little more than an hour…that would be on the clock…in fact 'I' was simply 'hanging in space.'

It was still storming when I gathered myself and wandered off to bed. I was tired…not the exhausted kind when you just flat run out of energy, but the kind you feel when you have been quietly 'filled' up and know that sleep will bring an extra bit of nourishing refreshment.

And so it was…

BE AND NOT SEEM

> "Go to the ant,…consider her
> ways, and be wise …"
> – Proverbs 6:6, <u>Bible</u>

The way we invest our time has everything to do with our quality of life. The things we think about and do, prepare us for the next unknown adventure. The way we invest our time helps us move forward in life.

Answering a couple of questions can help bring a little focus:
- What do you want out of life?
- How do you translate your desire into reality?

On the surface people might respond a new car, home, opportunities to travel and the like. But looking a little deeper, most say they just want to be happy…a little less tension and friction in their lives. Many of us experience our lives vicariously through books, television, movies and other time passing events. Yet, living passive lives bring us only temporary satisfaction, and as the years pass, before we know it, life has slipped by.

The writer of proverbs says:
> "A little extra sleep, a little more slumber, a little folding of the hands to rest—then poverty will pounce on you like a bandit; scarcity will attack you like an armed robber." – Proverbs 6:9-11

Most folk don't understand they can get the things they desire, take charge, and have some control over the quality of their lives. Most just show up each day and take whatever comes. This DOES NOT need to be the case.

Translating desire into action is the key, and developing positive habits goes a long way toward achieving one's goals. Marcus Aurelius puts it this way:

> "Early in the morning, when you are reluctant in your laziness to get up, let this thought be at hand: I am rising to do the work of a human being..." - Meditations

One good way to experience change is to think about others. Taking time to appreciate other people and having empathy for them, elevates our mood and increases the quality of our lives.

It has been written that it is better to give than receive. This isn't just good advice to help create a more harmonious culture; it is insight into a basic truth that growth and satisfaction happen when people share of themselves...of their time, energy, gifts and skills on consistent basis.

This is one of the great paradoxes of life...by giving with an open heart – no strings attached – we actually receive and grow. The good news is that this can be cultivated in daily life, with surprisingly little effort.

Try this experiment for the next month. Write five of the following items down on paper and put them on your bathroom mirror – this will keep them daily in front of you.

Look for an opportunity to try two or three of them every day. The next month, try a different two or three. You will be amazed at how simply your mood will be affected.

The exercises:

1. *Gratitude:* When you get up in the morning and put your feet on the floor, do it one foot at a time and say quietly out loud, "Thank you"...First foot touching, "Thank" – second foot touching, "you."
    • Do this every a day.

2. *Kindness*: At work, the store, with a neighbor or friend - say a kind word and smile.
• Try to do this five times in the day

3. *Empathy*: Look for someone in your life that is struggling, and tell them they are in your thoughts.
• Actively look for the opportunity

4. *Compliment*: Tell someone they look nice in their choice of clothing, cut of hair, loss of weight or any other small thing you notice.
• Do this at least twice a day

5. *Appreciate*: Let someone know you appreciate them – their spirit, the work they do, their friendliness, their wisdom in life or some other characteristic.
• As often as possible

6. *Thanks*: Tell someone they have done a good job – maybe a waitress, bus driver, colleague, husband, wife, significant other.
• At every opportunity

7. *Smile*: Smile at people when you see them or greet them (even if it is just in passing).
• Make this a habit

8. *Engage*: Ask someone about their life or interests or work. People love to talk about things important to them, and it is surprising what you can learn.
• This takes a little practice

9. *Help*: look for opportunities to help someone that could use it (e.g. open a door, carry a bag, put a grocery cart back for them).
• Whenever possible

10. *Do the unexpected*: Return too much change at the store, pick something up that a person dropped, open a door for someone, take someone for coffee or lunch.
• Try this once a month for yourself and someone else

THE BEAT GOES ON

"Be aware when things are out of balance…"
Lao Tzu – <u>Tao Te Ching</u>

"Stop philosophizing about what
a good man is and be one."
Marcus Aurelius - <u>Meditations</u>

The moment I stepped out of the room in tee shirt and light jacket, I knew I was in trouble. It wasn't actually 'the stepping out' of the room, but the millisecond it took to realize the key lay on the desk inside. You know the feeling – the mind gets it, but the hands not quick enough to beat the clicking sound of a securely shut door!

I was in the Ozark Mountains in Southern Missouri on my way to teach a course on the clinical management of chronic back pain. It was March and a great time to be in the 'Show Me' State. This is the time year, when the world begins waking from the winter, and the smell of impending spring fills the air like the expectant hope of the first flight of a young bird…a special anticipation to the air – ah, the cycle of life renewing itself once again!

The trip in had been uneventful and the motel, while modest, had one of those beds that afforded a great night's sleep. A common, but not excessive 'road warrior,' I have spent many a night in strange cities and in strange beds. No matter where the room, its cost, or what it looks like…<u>only one thing really matters</u> once the lights are out…<u>how does that bed sleep</u>! This one was excellent!

It was a modest, family-owned motel where the car parked just outside the room, so slipping out lightly clad seemed reasonable. Reason quickly faded as chilling reality took front seat. In addition to being outside the now locked door, the temperature had dropped twenty degrees over night bringing with it an unexpected snow and ice storm. It was very cold!

Clearly there was motivation to change my circumstance quickly. There is another motivating factor in the early morning hours – hot coffee! So rather than going to the office to get another key – a rational strategy – I fired up the car, turned on the defroster and waited, shivering until the car heated up – being an early riser doesn't imply common sense.

Coffee being the predominant thought, the hunt was on for an early morning vendor of that black elixir that renews the cycle of my life on a daily basis. This was, however, rural Missouri and it was going to take a little time to find a place.

You see what you look for - find what you know...
By the time I found the roadside restaurant, it was 5:30AM and the singular thought occupying my mind was that hot liquid of morning rebirth. The place was big and stark. The man behind the counter, in a tone of distracted non-interest said, "Do you want to smoke or not?" I said no and was pointed to a side room down a short hall.

The non-smoking room was a bit smaller with all but one table empty. Overhead, 1960s music was playing; the first couple that caught my attention were: "Help, I need somebody, help, not just anybody, help, you know I need someone. Help me," and "I can't get no satisfaction." – by the Beatles and Rolling Stones respectively. Songs that excited passion and debate in their day, but now seemed familiar, yet tired lyrics, reflecting a sense of paradise lost, with little help and a touch of thoughtful dissatisfaction. "Those were the days, my friend. We thought they'd never end…" Yet, like the slowly sinking sun into the Western sky, those days…those days slipped into the greyish unfocused shapes of yesteryears.

I was not alone…

I took an empty table and glanced at the others in the room. Both women already looked exhausted. They were mothers with three children between them – one baby and two little ones, each competing for attention – no men to be seen. The older of the two asked for a little more water apologizing for the mess the children were making. The waiter, no doubt having seen this movie more than once, said, "Sure" in a moderately inattentive and knowing monotone.

You could sense the mothers' anxiousness – these children needed to eat the food, because for them it was expensive and who knew what would be coming the rest of the day. How often growing up, did we hear variations of this expression, "Eat your food <*your name here*>. You should be grateful – just think of all the children starving in <*fill in the blank for the country*>."

The urgency and frustration in this disheveled, blue jean clad mother's voice, had little to do with starving children anywhere, but rather a compelling urgency that filling these children up was a necessity of life. Her words carried a tired sternness, "You need to eat the rest of your breakfast. Don't let me hear you say you are hungry later…" as if the child had anyway to understand the importance of fueling up for what might be the biggest – maybe only meaningful meal of the day.

The starkness of the scene, the sense of 'paradise lost' in the words of the tired 60s music, and the reality of millions of people living on the edge was overwhelming – almost tangible in this early morning hour. The emergent problems of these women were not my problems…or were they? The child caring, fatherless setting, all too common, even in this land where there is so much.

It is an old story…

What is the mother to do? How does she survive? Where does she find the resources to care for this unwanted, but clearly present responsibility? Who knows what she was thinking, or 'wanted to hear' when she was promised the "…whatever…" that caused her to 'give it up,' and led to this circumstance. She, of course, would do what mothers have done through all of time, when left to care from the *conception* and birth, of a *poorly conceived* moment in time. She would do whatever it took!

I got the coffee, had a little breakfast, paid my bill and added a tip. Yeah, I got a little more interested service, because it was clear, in this setting, only one table was going to tip anything, and it wasn't the women with the children.

One of us was inconvenienced by a minor unexpected circumstance, the consequence of which…get a new key and go on with the day – a small thing really. The others were inconvenienced by a grinding and unrelenting life circumstance - a much greater consequence. They wouldn't find a solution to their situation quite so easily.

What do we do? How do we '…pay it forward?' How do we invest the privilege we've been given to try and make a difference? Clearly, most of the world around us is out of our control, there is little we can influence other than our own thoughts, AND yet we can try to be good farmers…planting ideas and thoughts in the minds of those with whom we come in contact. We can also act on the thoughts that have been planted in our minds.

I should have quietly paid for their breakfast on my way out – I didn't. Next time I won't make the same mistake…lessons learned – hindsight, you know?

As I left the restaurant, I could hear the closing refrain of the Sonny and Cher hit echoing in my brain, "…the beat goes on, on, on, on, on…."

My hope? Today and next time - be a better man…

SOMETIMES YOU JUST HAVE TO WALK AWAY

"It's almost never the decision itself,
but the difficult path getting there."
- Anonymous

It's hard to know how the day is going to start. Yet as long as we have breath, each morning begins as it does for every living creature on the planet. Sometimes those days are predictable, but mostly they are not. This day things went badly...and went badly quickly.

The lioness escaped the sudden events that swiftly unfolded...her cub did not. In the aftermath, she looked around, and following a whimpering sound located her young offspring. The cub was not dead, but had been trampled by a herd of antelope or water buffalo or some other migrating pack that had been frightened by something unknown.

She came nuzzling and nudging the cub to move, but its lower back was broken – it could not. She picked it up in her mouth and carried it for a while. Whether it was the weight or fatigue or a combination...she put the cub down and slowly walked on. For a short period, it dragged itself along by its two front legs trying to keep up with its mother. She walked slowly allowing it to keep a distance of about ten feet between them. Then she stopped and sat...the cub paused, staring intently at her from behind.

The photographer had captured this rare and astonishing moment - the camera filming from the side as the drama played itself out. A second camera found itself positioned in full frontal view of the mother lion, sitting erect and regal – the cub plainly visible several feet behind her.

The war between the mothering instinct and struggle for survival appeared to be in play. The lioness seemed to be thinking… calculating… considering her options…running through some nameless decision making algorithm known only in her own mind. They say animals don't make subtle facial expressions, but watching her as she sat for those moments was riveting – the battle between the instinct of motherhood and for survival…almost in prayer.

Then something appeared to click in her mind. Something ancient…something primal…something tragic…a realization, a decision that telegraphed itself through the unseen camera directly into my heart. Like the arrow released from Paris' bow heading for Achilles' heel, there was no turning back…the endgame clear.

She glanced over her shoulder and looked directly at her cub…the fruit of her womb…the flesh of her flesh…and then turned to look straight ahead. She blinked her eyes, took a deep breath – a sigh really – and walked away.

It was one of the more profoundly moving and unexpectedly touching things I have seen in my life. It was not what I had expected. It was not the pleasant "…isn't that nice…" resolution to a potentially lethal situation. I did not smile at a satisfyingly haunting lyric like 'The Gambler' written by Don Schlitz; sung by the American artist Kenny Rogers:

> "You got to know when to hold 'em
> Know when to fold 'em
> Know when to walk away
> Know when to run…"

It was stark…real…life…death…decision…choice. All of that played out in a few astonishingly brief moments. In the most paradoxical of ways, the act was compassionately courageous. The mother had assessed the situation, tested the possibilities for survival, and made the most merciful decision for both she and her cub. The very rhythm of nature that brought the cub to life would now take it away…neither act either particularly willing or unwilling…simply a part of nature's 'what is.'

As human creatures in our culture, leaving our young would be unconscionable. As thinking social beings, we understand the future is not simply about our personal survival. We understand it is the transmission of conscious thought that builds the foundation, for our personal future, and that of our species. We understand we are, in fact, spiritual creatures housed in physical bodies…bodies, which in some cases not completely whole, hold the most wonderfully creative minds.

There are so many situations in life where we find ourselves unable to make decisions to move on from circumstances of hopelessness…the death of a loved one…the loss of a relationship…an abusive situation…the failure to succeed where time and energy has been spent.

The metaphor of choosing life, over the potential tragedy of two deaths, touched me deeply. Making conscious decisions, in spite of the difficulty in doing so, for a better life…a better future…all of that has played itself out in the theater of my mind since seeing that poignant video. Those few moments, calculated on the basis of the instinct for survival and choice for life, were profoundly touching.

"She blinked her eyes, took a deep breath – a sigh really – and walked away."

Lesson learned…

IT'S ABOUT THE BREATH

"It's easy to take for granted the breath that we breathe…
we forget that it is not a right, but a gift…"
- Author unknown

"It is never really the beginning of a thing that has the real meaning, but rather the end..."

You know the cliché; it's not about the destination, but the journey. While it may be true, if there is no journey, there will be no destination, 'end points' give meaning to the journey…they do give meaning, don't they?

"End points?" Are there really any? Isn't the end of one thing, just the beginning of another? Like breathing…the inspiration – breathe in…the expiration – breathe out…

Life doesn't just inspire and expire, but it respires…breath in and breath out in rhythmic cycles of a lifetime - each one of them critical in the moment. The moment…that is the key isn't it. That's what my yoga teachers have said. "Focus on the breath. It is all in the breath."

Breathing is so natural; we don't often appreciate the importance of the individual breath.

For all of the importance we place on the things we do, the things we create, the places we go…all of it…all of it hinges on the next breath. We conquer, build, negotiate, give birth, study, learn, create new worlds, and yet it all comes down to a single heartbeat…a single breath.

Focus on the breath…

The thing is, we have no guarantee for the next breath, and taking it for granted is not a good strategy. While it is not always the easiest thing to do, it is important to pay attention, or at the very least, respect the breath…because it provides the vehicle for further meaning in life.

Breathing is a metaphor for the people I know, the people I love, the relationships that bring meaning and rhythm to my life…the people that are easy to take for granted…like breathing…the people I simply expect to be there. This is not a good strategy, because one never knows when relationships will no longer have, or bring life.

I'm traveling this week – another city, another experience, another opportunity – yet in the quiet of my hotel this morning, I am focusing on my breath…the importance of the relationships, the care, the assurance, the faith my loved ones bring…the importance of keeping the quality of air in my lungs…the importance of not taking for granted their presence, nor 'their' breath.

Focus here is important because 'they' are what bring me life.

TEACHING OLD DOGS

> "That which *has been* is that which *will* be,
> And that which *has been* done is that
> which *will* be done. So there is
> nothing new under the sun."
> - Ecclesiastes 1:9: <u>Bible</u>

I'm taking a course!

It's a class on how to establish life habits for success. You know, the kind where you work through a structure that helps create a framework from which to motivate yourself to a more profitable and fulfilling life.

One could argue that developing successful life habits in one's sixties might just be a little late. After all, as my professional career and life, are on a gentle...maybe not so gentle downhill slope, shouldn't I be sharing life experience and lessons rather than trying to gather new ones?

That's the thing about lifetime learning, isn't it...you know, it just keeps going, until...well, the 'time of life' is over!

In addition, the concepts in this course are not new. In fact, as a person interested in the journey, there are not many new concepts to be heard. So why bother???

We are creatures of habit, and of little doubt, habit is built on certain principles that cultivate values, which in turn develop character...Yes sir, a lifetime of practicing habits is not a bad pursuit.

It is surprising, however, how easy it is to let certain things slip away because you think you already know them. For example, I tell my wife I love her every day. Do I think she doesn't know this? Am I concerned she might somehow forget? Not really. I do it because I realize how frail we really all are, and how frequently we need to be reminded of the things that matter.

> *Editorial comment:* A cautionary note – and trust me on this...I've learned words are not exactly like brushing one's teeth in the morning. My teeth do not care how I 'feel' about them...my wife does care how I 'feel' about her. So simply repeating words out of habit without paying attention...is not particularly wise.

I'll bet you like to hear people say your life is meaningful to them! There is little doubt I do.

Old/new...borrowed/blue...

Letting things slip by while we are pre-occupied is not new. Philosophic and religious literature is filled with ideas to guide our lives. Yet, these concepts remain as meaningfully fresh as the rising sun.

The parable of the different kinds of soil in the Bible is a favorite example. The seed sower tosses some seeds to the earth...landing on different soils – representing different aspects of our minds.

- Roadside soil: we hear and don't remember at all. Do you recall the information for that exam when you crammed all night? Of course you don't!
- Stony soil: words land in our minds, but don't take root...how about that diet or exercise program you started with enthusiasm? How did that go?
- Thorny soil: we get started doing something, but other priorities overcome them and we put them off...you know, that book you wanted to read or vacation you

thought would be good to take…

- <u>Good soil</u>: we focus on ideas that get exercised, which in turn produce new thoughts with more options to pursue…

The point? Think about things before jumping into them. Pay attention…count the cost at the beginning…measure twice, cut once…get the alphabet before writing the novel…

Cultivating words we hear have much to do with creating a workable framework within which to operate…that's what this life course is about.

For me?? It is the opportunity to 'check' the engine…to see how things are running.

Back to the point…
One of the assignments was to write a personal mission statement. Warm-up activities provided questions from which we were to write. For example, consider the different roles occupying your life: husband/wife, mother/father, uncle/aunt, neighbor, colleague, friend, and so on.

The next task, identify goals associated with the roles. For example, how would you like people, with whom you have these roles, to think about you? Were you honest, thoughtful, considerate, faithful and consistent…whatever was written.

Finally, we were to consider several people who influenced our lives (it could be anyone from any era). Invite them to an imaginary dinner and think about why they made the list.

Now we're getting somewhere…
The course provided examples of personal mission statements – some very short and some fairly long. My favorite short example: "I want to be the person my dog thinks I am." I have cats and therefore would make such a mission statement not particularly edifying!

I should say, at this juncture, it is not the first time I have written such a document…there was one in my late twenties and another in my mid-fifties. Both of them were long and wandering…attempting to distill things I felt were important.

They reflected those who had influenced my life…mentored and guided…disciplined and loved me. They spoke to the importance of character…consistency …virtue…justice – you know, the big things, and how I saw myself living in and interacting with the world. I wanted to be a better listener, consistent, trusted and seen as a person who finished what they started. I wanted to be a better man!

Nothing is straightforward…
The thing is that life is dynamic. It does not always present itself in black and white, and can be a painful reminder that "…the best laid plans of mice and…" mission statements often find themselves in conflict.

And so, it was helpful to go through the exercise once again for any number of reasons, not the least of which to take stock as to how I thought I was doing.

The lenses of life over time, like the eyes, need prescriptive adjustments. It's an odd thing though, unlike the eyes, with time life becomes clearer. The texture of the experiences lead one to consider each word and thought through a richer lens…that is the promise you know, "…if we ask, seek and knock…" we will see more clearly.

No more fooling around…
So, I dutifully wrote, and wrote, and wrote a little more – by the way, a meaningful exercise. In the end, however, the mission statement came down to this.

"Try to think of others first."

While a simple phrase, it was surprisingly difficult to distill everything I had written. It does encompass listening better, being consistent, mature and finishing things started.

The word "Try..." implies it is an ongoing process requiring daily reflection – a sharpening of the sword.

One would think this a revelation, but in fact, it is a principle invoked by those much wiser than I. My favorites...

- "...as you would that men should do to you, do you also to them likewise." – Christ: Luke 6:31
- "What I do not wish men to do to me, I also wish not to do to men." – Confucius: <u>Analectics</u>
- "...we are made for co-operation, like feet, like hands, like eyelids, like the rows of the upper and lower teeth. To act against one another is contrary to nature;... - Marcus Aurelius: <u>Meditations</u>

While the ideas are not new, the exercise was excellent! The good news? I'm not quite halfway through the course. Classes like this may not be the "...path less traveled," but they surely are great priority reminders...

The statement is done for the moment, the mission continues...

HOW ABOUT THOSE HANDS

"It's in the little things that life is made...
the smile, the touch, the kindness.
From the little become the great, and
greatness lies in these small acts."
- Anonymous

Have you noticed how it is the small things that so often make a difference? A knowing glance, a quiet nod of affirmation, a kind word, a polite gesture or a gentle touch – the little things that shape our life experience. It's said that when people know each other well; "...a smile is better than a word, a wink than a smile, and a nod than a wink..."

But the touch...ah the touch...now there is something. Little is more powerful than the human touch! Maybe that's why we have so many delicate sensory receptors in our fingers. Touch protects us from too much heat, cold, things that are too sharp, and permits us to sense the correct pressure to firmly shake a person's hand or gently pick up a fragile egg.

Of the primary senses in the fingers, pressure has the most receptors. Take a moment to brush your thumb gently across your fingertips noticing the pressure and sensation. Then run the fingers of one hand lightly down the palm side fingers of the other hand – note the difference between the two activities. Now close your eyes and softly touch your face – forehead, cheeks, eyebrows, lips and nose – sense the differences in texture.

Touch…what a gift!

While touch does have a 'reporting function' – heath, cold, pressure and pain – it is NOT just the colliding of electrons from skin to skin, or skin to object, that brings the real magic to this sensory phenomenon. There is much more than meets 'the touch' as it were.

Touching another person, for example, can be a wondrous sensory experience. There is little doubt that the one touching and the one receiving both feel a sense of heightened connection. It's hard to find something more satisfying and sometimes more intimate, than the loving caress from the hand of one person to another.

More than a physical phenomenon

In the scriptures, Christ finds himself amongst a large crowd of people. He says to his disciples, "Who touched me?" One of them, with a '…*you have got to be kidding me*…' expression replies, "…there is a crowd of people around you – bumping, pushing – and you are asking who touched you!" Jesus responds, "…**somebody** hath **touched me**: for I perceive that virtue is gone out of me…" (Luke 8:46)

A lot of people were touching Christ physically, but *someone* had *touched him spiritually* AND taken something from him – a transfer of spirit from Christ's spiritual body to a woman, and she was healed.

It is a spiritual thing

It could be argued that fingers and touch are a metaphor for something deeper – a channel of communication – a conduit whereby spirit is transferred from one person to another. It slips through the skin, muscle, bone, and **reaches the soul**. Touch transcends the physical – it really is spiritual in every way.

Sometimes when we hear Biblical and other miraculous reports that happen to people, we think of it as strange; it even makes some people uncomfortable. In a real sense, it is about the laying on of hands. This isn't something limited to the realm of spirit filled Pentecostal or Evangelical people….we all do it every day in the most common of ways – a shake of the hand, a pat on the back, or a 'high-five.'

Everybody '...lays on hands...'

Many parents tell stories of how a distraught child was calmed when taken in their arms. This was simply transferring peace or assurance from parent to child through the laying on of hands. A soothing word of course helps, but it is the touch that counts.

As adults, we all identify with times when we were fortified by a pat on the arm or a brief hug in a moment of need. It doesn't even have to be a moment of need. Maybe it's just the greeting to a friend or family member. It is just nice to receive an affirmation by human contact that comes in this way.

Athletes understand how important a thoughtful slap on the shoulder, from a teammate or coach, returns the spirit of confidence for their game.

It is instinctive that we reach out to touch those who find themselves in need – even more so toward those with whom we have a bond – those we love and care about.

A pair of docs!

The paradox of modern society is that we have been provided with so many things intended to make the quality our lives better. Computers do a lot of work previously done by hand, cell phones allow us to talk from practically anywhere, and texting messages can keep us in instantaneous contact with short bursts of information. In an unfortunate way, these labor saving devices have allowed us to better communicate information, but do not provide the kind of spiritual exchange we get from that profoundly subtle and sometimes not so subtle gesture of physical/spiritual human contact.

Sometimes less is more; being physically present with others is much more helpful than a call or text. In spite of this kind of communication being fairly recent, it is instructive to note that even the ancients appreciated the importance of the bond of the universal human family.

"Consider often the connection of all things in the Cosmos and their relationship with each other. For in a way all things are actually intertwined, and thus according to this there is a natural inclination, or love that links everything together... " Aurelius M <u>Meditations</u>

For all the ways we communicate, without being present with one another, there is nothing like touch to engage our senses when we are together. It is our nature to work together. Withholding sensory communication from one another is against the nature we have been given.

Remember touch…it's the little things – they are huge!

THE CLOCK IS TICKING

"If you're always battling against getting older, you're always going to
be unhappy, because it will happen anyhow."
Schwartz, M – Tuesday's with Morrie

The clock ticks and another minute expires, slowly, with the
unrelenting deliberateness of a glacier grinding its way down a
mountainside. The seconds' fly, but minutes move imperceptibly
from one to the next…and the next…and the next…

On this day…exactly the moment of this post (1300Z GMT or
0900 EDT), I will have repeated this cycle 33 million, 6 hundred 38
thousand, 400 times. That's a lot of minutes.

We are not used to thinking in these increments of time; they
seem, well…too much minutiae. Yet as the "…journey of a thousand
miles begins with the first step…" countless minutes pile up
providing a framework that permits each of us to become the person
we are.

Minutes – in the big picture – seem relatively meaningless.
Meaningless may not be correct, but barring unexpected death or
terminal illness, we have millions of them to spend.

"The days of our years are threescore years and ten;
and if by reason of strength they be fourscore years, yet
is their strength labour and sorrow; for it is soon cut
off, and we fly away…" (Psalms 90:10 – Bible)

We work through them, fight through them, sing through them, dance through them, love through them, sleep through them and do all manner of things to occupy our lives through them.

Birth – death...(taxes?)

While it is easy to lose track of the minutes in our lives, two are particularly meaningful. In the oddest of ways, while significant in the extreme – in the moment, their importance is completely lost on us.

The first minute signals the beginning, as we emerge from the womb with life and its unpredictability lying in front of us. We gasp for the thin atmosphere of air so alien from the amniotic fluid that moved in and out of our lungs in our mother's womb. We do not remember this event, but family and close friends preserve memories of that promising entrance into life. Mothers cherish the miraculous fruit of their labor – the marvel of childbirth renewing the cycle of life - refreshed yet again.

Once that breath is taken, the clock begins ticking – minute after relentless minute toward the second truly extraordinary and meaningful minute and breath...our last! Everything in between is the lyric and music that brings meaning to our life experience.

A momentary pause...

Each stage of life happens only once. As infants we're weak and need support; as children structure and education. We are impulsive and spontaneous in youth, serious and thoughtful in middle age and hopefully mature and reflective in old age...each of these seasons bear some sort of fruit – gathered and stored for the next stage.

This idea becomes more important as one edges into old age. What is old age anyway? Surely it comes after middle age, but where is that invisible line?

It has been said 60 years (31 million minutes and change) is the new 40. It is not clear to me what that means either. Over the years, it always seemed strange to hear people I knew resist (as if they could) entering their 30s and 40s as though they were somehow toxic. There must be a marker or measurement somewhere that I missed as the decades have come and gone.

I have got to be honest here, as I rose the morning following my 30th, 40th, 50th and 60th birthdays, I felt pretty much the same as I had the day before. It should also be noted, except for the inability to jump as high, run as fast or hold my breath as long, the passing of this 63rd year as I write, has been the best of my life…as were the previous years when I was living them.

Back to the minutes…

While each of us is somewhat different, the time course of life – barring an unforeseen event – is fixed. Nature, which constructed the unimaginably intricate body in which we live, as if to say, "…this time is enough…" deliberately and thoughtfully deconstructs our lives…easing us toward the unavoidable end of earthly experience. It is the natural order of things, the rhythm of life repeated billions of times, not something to be feared – rather embraced.

That first minute, begins with a blank slate…the last minute, preceded by adventure after adventure, passes as we leave behind all that we have known. In the most profound of ways, we are curiously clueless about both. We share neither excitement of the beginning of our lives, nor sorrow of the departure from it. We, the principle character in the play, are given little insight into either event. We only gain a little understanding by witnessing the birth or death of others. It is even ironic that we celebrate the battle and struggle to begin life and sorrow for the final peace that we all seek.

The final breath occurs as we fight to maintain the life that began so many uncounted minutes before…the last breath – the 'agonal gasp' as it is called, signals a close to the journey – a shedding of the physical skin…leaving all behind.

Old age?

If I am approaching old age (as part of the 'new 40s'), I am grateful there is no indication as to when that last minute and breath will occur. Since it is clear that it will happen and there is nothing to be done about it, I can set that aside and get on with everything I possibly can out of life…embracing it as it comes. At this time of life, there is better focus and a cutting away of the distractions of earlier years...because this time of life permits paying attention to the things that have more meaning to me.

While "I...have repeated this cycle 33 million, 6 hundred 38 thousand, 400 times," I know a couple of things:

1. If my last minute and breath were to occur as this post is sent, I could not have asked for a better and more quality life experience. Having said that...
2. I'm looking forward to a few million more!

SUBWAYS IN BERLIN

> "The robbed that smiles, steals
> something from the thief."
> Shakespeare - <u>Othello</u>

Sometimes you get a win when you didn't even know you were in the game.

She was about five years old holding her mother's hand when they got on board.

The setup...

The subway car had been full when I climbed on ten stops earlier...full of commuters heading home for the day. I was in Europe for a conference and had a little time to see the city. It was Berlin and I had just finished 10 hours of visiting museums and getting around the city to find them...I was really tired – the kind where you have reached the edge of your brain's capacity to absorb another piece of information and your 64 year old body is asking, "What were you thinking!?" You know what I mean.

I hopped on the subway at *Mehringdamm* station - well, not exactly 'hopped' – for the 18-station trip to my hotel near the *Rohrdamn* station. I had taken a seat facing backward across from a young man listening to his iPod, completely oblivious to me or anyone else – his head moved to a beat only he could hear. You have no doubt heard the saying attributed to Friedrich Nietzsche: "*...those who were seen dancing were thought to be insane by those who could not hear the music.*" This would describe him exactly...it was nice to see this young man in doing his own thing and in his own world.

As the people thinned out, a bench facing forward opened up across the Isle; I slipped over and settled in with a little more legroom. All four seats (two forward and two backward) were open except for the place I had taken by the window.

The event…

The little girl got on at *Wilmersdorfer* with her mother who was pushing her to sit facing backward, directly across from me. It was a seat by the door and would be an easy 'on' and 'off.' I'm a pretty big fellow, and the girl looked a little unsure about sitting across from me, but was obedient in the rush and sat down. She was tiny, as most five year olds are, cute with a knee length jumper and full length, brightly colored stockings.

I looked over and noticed she was staring at me. I caught her eye, and she did what most children do when caught glancing at a stranger, she looked quickly down. We rode together for 3 stops to *Mierendorflpl* with four stops left for me, when I noticed she was carrying a small plastic bag in her right hand. Through the plastic, I saw a 5"x7" (15x18cm) portrait 'head shot' of the little girl. As she nervously turned the plastic back and forth, I could see another picture of several children posing for the camera – a class picture from her school.

The train was just pulling into the station when I pointed to the picture and then to her, raising my eyebrows and smiling. This is, by the way, my international sign language for short messages with children. It was all I had…I don't speak German! She nodded, grinned brightly…a warmth that could have lit the afternoon sun with a full 'tooth showing' smile – we connected!

The payoff…

As she and her mother got off the train, I wondered with a little anticipation…had the magic between us worked? She trotted off toward the exit holding her mother's hand, and then it happened…she turned to see if I was watching – we connected again – her smile widened and she waved the little hand that was holding the pictures of she and her classmates – A WIN!!

In that moment, all the tiredness of the day slipped away. The unspoken and knowing connection between two human beings had occurred in one of the great languages of the soul…the open smile. It did not require a hard earned vocabulary, hours of repetitive practice, nor finding a place for subtle expression in written or spoken thought – No! The only elements necessary for this to happen were proximity (being near one another) and a willing heart. The scriptures says, "…if first there be a willing mind…" All things are possible and in that moment the universe was working well.

On that day, in that city, sitting exhausted on that subway car, I was once again reminded of how much we all are alike…young-old, tall-short, black-white-yellow-red…we are connected by the fabric of humanity, and when that connection happens, WE KNOW this is the way God intended for life to be for all of us, if we just take the time to listen and be refreshed.

The smile from that little girl, was more rewarding in the moment, than all the reading, listening and watching I have done in my life, to try and understand what any of this life means. That little girl, in that moment, reminded me that we can share with each other the most profound of things, in the lightening briefness when two souls touch through the magic of a shared smile.

DOWNS - NOT OUT

"Relax," said the night man,
"We are programmed to receive.
You can check out anytime you like,
But you can never leave!"
- Felder, Frey, Henley:
Hotel California

"Honey…honey," she squealed as she saw me come around the corner.

She charged down the hall with that hallmark unstable gait that made her look like she was going to fall over sideways with every step. She threw her arm around my legs, stood on my feet and hugged me for all she was worth.

When I arrived on the unit, there was little doubt Shelley was 'my' girl…my girl.

It was the late 1970s, in the second year of my doctoral program, and I was taking a course that required I spend a couple of nights a week at the university hospital pediatric cancer ward.

The blessing – the curse…
I have always had the capacity to not over think coming events in my life. This has been a gift, and sometimes a curse. It was a gift in the military, meaning I simply got up each day and faced whatever had been planned for me. Basic training, okay…specialty training, that was fine…Vietnam, let's do it… Since there was little I could do

about the system, this attitude minimized my stress levels. It has also been the same in matters of the heart for me. Don't over think…go with the flow.

In the military, this gift served me well – I survived. In matters of the heart, I have soared to the mountaintop and been crushed in the "…valley of the shadow of death!!" Of little doubt a curse.

The circumstance…

My task wasn't very complicated. I showed up Tuesday and Thursday evenings for an hour and a half and played games with children, who for the most part would never see puberty. I have always liked youngsters, so I thought this might be a good experience.

These kids were all somewhere between seven and eleven, and for the most part looked pretty much the same. Shaven heads…sallow skin…no longer any self-consciousness…the brightness and sparkle in their eyes adding a visual contradiction that they were all terminal cancer children. Of little doubt, they were '…dead kids walking…'.

They had the look of a future race of from a science fiction film, but this was no fantasy. Each of them had a death warrant, and as they slipped away one by one, their loss brought closure <u>and</u> sorrow to the families upon whom this terminal sentence would be equally shared.

Equally?? Not so equally, for <u>it is</u> the living who carry this forward, isn't it??

The task at hand…

They were surprisingly enthusiastic when I showed up. There was a box filled with board games for the older ones, some balls and small toys for the younger. I told a story each evening and brought my guitar to sing a song or two, because…well, I didn't know what else to do. I felt somehow out of my element, but they had a kind of wisdom and a surprising amount of loving tolerance, which made me feel, by the end of most evenings together, that my visits were meaningful.

I had actually compartmentalized this pretty well. I knew they were terminal, and when I arrived for an evening and one of them had lost the battle, I was saddened, but seemed to be able to handle it and go on – you know, above the fray…or so it seemed. However, the cumulative affect of these children's deaths would haunt me for years. I mean, what was the point?

The unexpected…

But then there was Shelley…damn! Somehow she got under my skin and traveled through the circulatory system of my spiritual body, lodging herself firmly in my heart. Something happened in my tenure at this "…hotel California…" that touched me so deeply, that as I write these words so many years later, tears gently fall.

Shelley had Down's Syndrome, and in addition to all the complications that can happen to a child born with this disorder, she had terminal cancer. Often these kids are intellectually impaired, have seizures, hearing loss, visual deficiencies, upper respiratory problems and a host of other issues. Shelley had them all, and a little more. In addition to this, she was a behavioral problem!

The biggest difficulty was her incontinence. As a result she was kept in a diaper, which she hated! The nurses would put them on her and she would take them off. Shelley was 10, of fair size and stubborn with a capital 'S!' Keeping her in diapers was problematic.

One evening, I suggested to the charge nurse they put her in panties rather than the diaper to see what she would do. For some reason known only to the gods, she put panties on the girl and Shelley never soiled herself again! While she had cognitive problems, she wasn't stupid. What she really wanted – and could not express – was to simply be like the other girls.

Love at third sight…

By the second or third week of my 16-week tenure at the hospital, I had fallen hopelessly in love with this quirky little girl, who ran to me without fail every time I entered the children's ward. Her glasses never stayed squarely on her face…she enjoyed making bodily sounds – laughing out loud – and almost always smiled when she looked at me. Like any situation of the heart, I cannot really say what it was or how it happened, but from that point forward I was her "…Honey, Honey…"

I found myself looking forward to those evenings. No matter how difficult Shelley had been during the day or week, when I showed up, she would calm down and become a model patient. Neither the nurses nor I were sure what caused this, but they also looked forward to my visits.

Just before Christmas of that year, Shelley needed bowel surgery. She had obstructed and they went in to remove the blockage. I stayed with her that night at the hospital. She was still medicated, but would open her eyes from time to time and look to see if I were still there. She would smile and quietly say, "…honey, honey…" We held hands and she would drift away, only to open her eyes again, smile and utter those words.

She survived the surgery, much to my delight and I headed home for Christmas break. I thought of her quite a bit those couple of weeks at home and picked up a little present for her. I had been surprised how special and natural it had become for us to see one another. I made a decision to continue to visit her, even though my assignment was finished.

Back from the holiday…
I got back to school on the weekend and headed to the hospital to see how my girl was doing. When I entered the ward, the charge nurse came to me, put her arms around me and softly said, "Shelley didn't make it…complications from the surgery. She died over the holidays." I was stunned…had I not been in this woman's arms I'm not sure I would have been able to stand. This, of course, was not possible…this was Shelley…my girl!

That night the entire nursing staff from the day shift took me out to console me. They had lots to say about their work and their families and I realized, while I was a small cog in the wheel of their lives, my time there had meant something. I remember that evening with a sense of bittersweet gratitude for these heroic people whose profession was daily filled with loss.

It's been more than 36 years since that little girl captured my heart, yet every time I think of her my thoughts drift to some magic place where I am sure she is free…where I realize how little it really takes when the spirit is clean and the love pure.

Every once and awhile, in the quiet of the night, she comes like an ill-gaited fairy princess, stumbling down the hallway of my mind to wrap her arms around the legs of her prince…a moment of secure love…a little time with her "…honey, honey…"

CANADIAN SUMMERS

"In youth, it was always the place not the people.
Time so changes one's perspective, for
in old age, it was never the place..."
-anonymous

South Central Ontario, Canada in the summer... there was a time when only God and a special few knew her.

More properly it was the Muskoka (Mus-ko-ka) region of Ontario that had attracted folk by its pastoral scenery and astonishingly beautiful lakes. There were three that were linked together: Lakes Muskoka, Rosseau (Ross-so) and Joseph.

Ah Joseph, like its biblical name's sake, this was a lake of richly deep and clear waters, around which in the fall, its mantle of hardwood leaves defined the very essence of God's vivid imagination – a cloak of such festive colors even Joseph himself would have felt some envy.

Before my time...
In the early 1900s my grandfather owned an art supply store in Toronto. He was looking for a place to deposit the family in the summers while he went to Europe to buy brushes and other items for his inventory. How he discovered this land, is unknown to me, but find it he did. He purchased 212 acres (85.7 hectares) on the northeastern shores of Lake Joseph. Lakes Muskoka and Rosseau had been found and occupied with summer hotels and cottagers for many years, but the Northern end of Lake Joe was more difficult to

get to and had remained relatively untouched.

Buying the land was one thing, getting there another. My mother talked about how they would take the train from Toronto to Bala – some 120 miles (193km) – and wind their way to Port Sandfield, a small town at the confluence of Lakes Joseph and Rosseau. They would then fill a small motor driven 'putter boat' and make their way up the 10 or 11 mile (16-17.7km) journey to Stanley Bay where the land lay.

The original cottage was a log cabin in a clearing around 100 yards (91 meters) or so from the lakeshore. Twelve of the acres were on the lakeshore, while the back 200 contained a ten acre (4 hectares), beaver inhabited lake and uncharted woods.

Summers were spent playing in the water and surrounding areas, while working to keep the raccoons and other small animals from raiding the pantry of food. Every couple of weeks, a supply boat would come to a wharf about a quarter of a mile up the shoreline, where they purchased supplies, and I understand, an occasional candy bar.

My era...
By the time I arrived on the planet, the land had been in the family for nearly 37 years. A family cottage had been built along the shore, in the middle of the 12 acres that kissed the southern edges of Stanley bay. Family members would reserve time in the summers to take the cottage for a few weeks of campfires, corn roasts, sing-songs, fishing, Sunday church and interaction with whatever creatures of the woods ventured by to see these odd two-legged hairless animals.

There was no electricity, no indoor plumbing, no telephone, no television...just family, a few board games we all played and our imaginations to fill the seemingly never-ending days that melted into cool, blanket hugging nights.

It was during these years when family members began branching out to build their own cottages along the quarter mile (402m) shoreline. One of my uncles had purchased the beach at the end of the bay, so it could be argued the end and entire southeastern shoreline of the bay was in family possession.

My mother was assigned a section of land, and my father began, what would become better than a decade's odyssey of building our family cottage. As a carpenter, my dad was a pretty good minister. To say he had building skill, would be the grossest of overstatements. While he served that great carpenter from Bethlehem and Nazareth, his enthusiasm exceeded his skill by a large margin. Dad was a minister of the Gospel. The 'cottages' he built for a living were "…not made with hands." Yet he was undeterred.

Every summer, he would borrow a little money, purchase small amounts of building materials and spend the month of August building our cottage. Finally, on a day of celebration and great excitement we moved from the family cottage into our very own place along the bay. There would be no more haggling for cottage time…we could be there whenever we wanted.

Thirty days a year…
Our holiday was the month of August, and we always had a lot of people visit. Rarely a day or two went by where someone would not show up from somewhere. It was truly 'mi casa – es su casa' (my home is your home). If we didn't have more than 50 souls visit during that month, my mother felt she had done something wrong.

Food, from the general store, was delivered a couple of times a week. I would provide fresh fish for breakfast whenever I was lucky enough to catch some.

The family routine was pretty well set. The evenings were generally social gatherings in the living room. We played games, told stories, laughed at silly jokes and…and…and we were circled in a love and fellowship that seemed so normal. I didn't realize they were set in motion deliberately by parents who understood the importance of community and hospitality. We learned these life skills as naturally as young children learn a foreign language.

Nights and days...

Each night dad would lay the next morning's firewood. Both he and mum were early risers, and as dad lit the morning fire, mother would be in the kitchen singing quietly to herself while she got breakfast ready. She was the ultimate optimist; if dealt a poor hand, she would make something out of it.

A lot of people from many different cultures, nations and belief systems came to the Dreisinger cottage over the years. We were encouraged to bring our friends or invite acquaintances - who, in the end, could not fail to become in some way, a part of our extended family. It was a laboratory of hospitality that prepared us for ways in life we could never imagine.

Cottages are great, but mothers...

One of my favorite stories, and one my friend John has reminded me of from time to time involved some fellas from Africa that came for a short visit. He brought them to the cottage, and they only had a couple of days to be with us. I had pumped up the idea of going out on the lake and doing some fishing. The smaller lake on the property, in addition to having beaver, also had lots of frogs that could be used for bait. We spent a day catching them and digging for worms. I could hardly wait!

The next morning, a huge thunderstorm unexpectedly appeared, meaning we weren't going to be doing anything but staying in the cottage, with me sulking. I was particularly upset as I crossed the living room toward the kitchen ready to complain my heart out to mother. As I got near the door, I heard her quietly singing to herself as she got breakfast ready for the small herd that was visiting. This was her custom in the mornings. This particular morning it was one of her favorite hymns: JL Hall's "When morning gilds the skies."

The tune is gently melodic, and the words of the first verse begin like this:

"When morning gilds the skies
my heart awakening cries:
May Jesus Christ be praised!

Alike at work and prayer,
to Jesus I repair:
May Jesus Christ be praised!"

The skies were darkened with clouds, rain and thunder and my mother was singing about the sun coming to the morning sky. My heart was stung by the contrast between my gloomy mood and the talent she had for keeping her disposition elevated. When I entered the kitchen, she could feel my frustration. She just smiled, said she loved me, and asked if I would begin setting the table. She had a skill set that it would take me decades to learn, one in all honesty I have not fully mastered.

As I have gotten older and benefited from the lessons of my youth, I have read lots of life enhancing things. The scriptures have been a place of comfort for me...I enjoy a little history and philosophy for reinforcement...I embrace the laboratory of life, where the next moment is sometimes so unexpected as to take my breath away. BUT if I really want to settle my heart, and find that place of quiet strength, I close my eyes and see my mother standing in front of the sink at the cottage gently singing to herself... "When morning gilds the skies..."

JUST A GAME

"All life is an experiment. The more
Experiments you make, the better."
- Emerson, R.W.

His name was Fredrick Keith, but everyone knew he was 'Freddy Freeze.' Yes sir, as a basketball handler, none of us had ever seen anyone the likes of Freddy. In a close game with just a little time on the clock and a narrow lead, Freddie Freeze ALWAYS took the ball!

Military life winding down...

It was 1970 at Ft. Rucker, Alabama. The war was over for some of us and we were spending our last year doing our military jobs before leaving the service. I was living in a trailer with my best friend Dave, and 'Widetrack' the dog.

We hung around with a few fellas, but it was late summer and I needed more than my part-time bar waiter's job at the Officer's Club to keep myself busy. As has been so often the case in my life, the unexpected happened. Even though I lived off base, an occasional Saturday morning would find me in the gym shooting basketball.

Game on...

One of these mornings, the Ft. Rucker post basketball team was practicing. It was the beginning of the season and they were working on drills. The team was a half and half mix of white and African American players. I can't exactly recall how it happened...maybe it was a shoot around...maybe it was they were asking around for another player or two...However it happened, I found myself on the

52

team. A captain was the coach and it turned out all the white players, except me, were officers.

My first preseason game was with a local Community College...I warmed the bench. Interestingly, so did the black players. We all sat and watched the officers get their clocks cleaned by a group of local junior college wannabes. I thought we had a great mix of players on the squad, but it was 1970, we were in the Deep South, I was a Northern boy and frankly – naïve.

It wasn't that I hadn't experienced racial prejudice. In fact, once I had to buy food for a couple of my high school teammates when we played junior varsity basketball in Grafton, West Virginia. We had finished an afternoon game before the varsity played, and left the gym to grab something to eat. The small restaurant wouldn't serve my teammates...I bought the food and we sat outside on the curb and ate the hotdogs. Hot dogs! Yeah, but it <u>was</u> the 60s.

We played a couple more games at our home gym before the season actually started. I got a few minutes of play as did the black players, but on balance, the officers played...and lost. What we didn't know was the post commander had come to watch, and was apparently unhappy with the results of 'his' team.

Life is change...
We practiced every afternoon at the Post Gym for a couple of hours. After the third loss, the complexion of the team changed with the suddenness of monsoon rains turning a sunny skies into a downpour of unrelenting rain. That afternoon none of the officers showed up for practice. In fact, neither did the coach.

We started our normal shoot around to warm up, wondering whether we had '...missed the memo...,' when a short red headed first lieutenant, with a drop-dead gorgeous woman by his side, came in the gym and called the team together. As quickly as the door slammed in the faces of Eva Duarte de Perón's rejected lovers, the captain was gone and Lieutenant Miller became our new coach.

Miller announced, he had never played basketball, didn't know the game and was nervous about this assignment. So nervous, he had brought his wife along for moral support. We were stunned by our new coach AND his attractive wife. It was one of those moments of cognitive dissonance – you know, our coach knew nothing about the game (not so good), but his wife was really attractive (not so bad)!

The commanding General felt there was a lot of talent on the team that wasn't being properly used, and so with the swiftness of a dropping guillotine blade, made the change. From that day forward, we never saw our old coach or any of the officer players again!

Then there was Freddy...

Miller asked how many guys had played college ball...five of the six African American players had college degrees and had started for their respective basketball teams. Freddy Keith? Well Freddy had played playground basketball in New York City. For the uninitiated, New York street basketball is some of the best played anywhere on the planet...and we had an authentic NYC play grounder on our team!

Freddy had not originally been on the team, but was well known as the best player on base. Unfortunately, he was also known as a significant troublemaker. Outside of the gym, he had been a real problem, and in spite of having been in the military for almost three years, he was still a private first class – the lowest ranking enlisted man outside of basic training. He had been busted more times than a professional lady of the night working Times Square in his beloved New York City!

The only thing that saved him from being put in the post stockade was the ingenuity of his company commander, who out of sheer frustration told Freddy that if he got into any more trouble, the post gym would be off limits. A stroke of genius! Freddy coveted the game so much that the threat of losing gym privileges put him on the straight and narrow. He had '...found the Lord...' and a starting guard position on the team.

It is hard to express the beauty of a gift that has been worked and worked, until it becomes sharper than the scalpel of a world-class surgeon. This was Freddie's ability with the basketball. It was only a game, but it was 'his' game. Never before or since…in collegiate or professional play…have I ever seen someone handle a basketball with the skill, focus, and, yes, love in the way Freddie played the game. His only reward? To be allowed in the gym to play the game.

The roster was filled…

We picked up another white guy, who had played some college ball somewhere in the northern plain states…a forward with a sweet shot and deadly accuracy from anywhere between 20 and 30 feet. That was it…eight of us – a brotherhood of young men who loved the game, and in the end each other.

What Miller lacked in knowledge he made up for with unrelenting enthusiasm and a humbly pragmatic mind for delegation. He knew…we knew – but no one else, that he had virtually no knowledge of the game…we NEVER spoke about it. He assigned specialist 4th class John P. to captain the team. Miller would be the 'coach' – John would design and call the plays. It was an unspoken reality that served us well.

The mandate from the Post Commander had been simply this – WIN! How and with whom didn't matter to him…a black team – a white team…he didn't care – just win! The only thing that seemed clear…it would not be an officer team.

It was meaningful…

I learned a lot of basketball in those games with those men. I was the highest jumper on the team thanks to the large 'rear end' and strong thighs my mother had given me. I got a starting role – not because I was white, but because I could jump and had excellent rebound timing (Mum again). To this day, I cherish the starting slot on that team as one of the great joys and achievements of my life….no token place in this brotherhood – you made the grade or someone else did.

Because we were a post team we traveled all over the south playing other military Base and Fort teams. We also had a girls' team that traveled with us on the road. They actually didn't travel with us, but we often double-billed at home and away games. They were all African American and they loved me! When I say they loved me, I mean I was the starting white boy, the anomaly, and they cheered their hearts out whenever I scored or defended well. It was at that time in my life I learned to love women's basketball, and the women who play it.

I was the only guy on the team with a military drivers license, so I chauffeured for all the away games. I actually can't remember how many games there were that season, nor how close the finishes were. I do remember watching Freddy taking us through the final buzzer more than once with the magic glue of fingertips from which even triple teaming opponents could not remove the ball.

When it was all said and done, we lost only one game that season…it was the divisional championship against Fort Campbell, and it was close. We weren't the biggest (I was center at 6'5" – 1.95m), nor were we the fastest. We were a team of young men who learned to love *Lieutenant Miller* for his openness and enthusiasm…*John P.* for his leadership and strategic mind designing plays that worked…*each other* for the selfless play of the game…AND our secret weapon – Freddy 'the freeze' Keith!

I also learned a few life lessons that year on that team:

- Generals can do whatever they want
- Creative leadership makes a difference in people's lives
- Success happens best when it doesn't matter who gets credit
- When people focus on the task at hand, prejudice has little place
- Some people are so gifted you would rather 'watch them play,' than play with them!
- Love may not conquer all, but when done right, it can surely satisfy the soul

In the quiet moments as I write this piece, and reflect on that group of nobody guys…on a nobody team…in a no place part of the country, what a rich part of my life that was. There was no hometown loyalty, no crowds of friends and family attending the games…there was us and the bond of the game.

We live such a short span of life, and really only in the present moment. Everything not in the moment is either past or yet unknown. In this moment, I have chosen to reflect on one of the small nooks and crannies of my life…briefly replaying the feelings toward those men, and running the tapes of the artistry of Freddie Freeze.

In quite moments that start my days, it doesn't get much better than that.

LIFE AND THE DESERT

"Once again there was the desert,
and that only."
- Stephen King, <u>The Gunslinger</u>

"Wear light colored clothing to reflect the sun; take plenty of water…drink it before you get thirsty; wear a broad brimmed hat to protect your head AND the back of your neck; never put your hand somewhere where you cannot see."

These are basic instructions when hiking in the desert – a good place to start…a few simple guidelines.

There are people who know these things…people who have learned through experience, that nature has no conscience – it has a rhythm, that when honored, makes it a wonderful place to visit. When dishonored or ignored, can be dangerous…sometimes lethal. Following a few basic instructions can make a desert experience safer and enjoyable. Unexpected challenges might – probably will – occur, but an "…ounce of prevention…" is surely "…money in the bank…" toward the solution of an unexpected problem! If you are respectful, it is a spectacularly beautiful place.

The Anza-Borrego desert, in San Diego County, is a hot place in the summer – as high as 107 degrees (41.6C). One would think in this kind of heat, with sand and rocks everywhere, that it would be a desolate place…one would be wrong!

The desert is absolutely teeming with life. There are innumerable cactus, bushes and small scrub trees. There is life almost everywhere, from the tiniest of lizards, spiders and broad varieties of insects, to birds, coyotes, jackrabbits, big horn sheep and the occasional mountain lion. They say the mountain lions typically stay away from people unless they are desperately hungry. They say if you come across a desperately hungry mountain lion...well, it just isn't your day! Yes sir, if you miss that mountain lion, and take a few precautions, the desert is about as interesting a place as you could imagine!

Borrego Springs is a small town sitting on the northwestern edge of the Anza-Borrego desert. It gets its name because of the natural source of water coming from underground to sustain this community, and as you drive down the winding mountain road leading to the desert floor, the brownish colored basin is dotted with patches of green where there is naturally occurring water.

Let's do this...
This past week I was in the desert for a few hours with a newly discovered friend – the son of a close friend from Denmark. He had just finished a year as an exchange student a little north of Los Angeles, and came to spend a few days. Since the deserts in Denmark are very small - in fact, practically impossible to find – it seemed like a good idea to give him an idea what a real desert is like! Our goal – a 3mile (4.8km) round trip hike, in a canyon, to a spring surrounded by a grove of palm trees.

It was 97 degrees (36C) when Andreas and I got to the trailhead at 9am. We were prepared...the water, the hats, the clothing. As we started out, a group of locals were just finishing their morning hike, and a fellow with three children from Virginia were just getting ready to head out on the trail.

The locals? They were done by 9am, because they knew the best war is the one not fought...they understood and were finished before the day got really hot.

The family from Virginia? They were wearing dark clothing, and only the dad had a hat — a black baseball cap. I mentioned to them, how quickly one can lose body water in the desert and how hats might be helpful. He smiled politely, indicated they would be okay, and gently dismissed my concerns. What can you do?

Off we went. There were two trails in…one was fairly easy…the other a little more challenging. We took the fairly easy one in…the more difficult one out. It was a 45 minute hike each way.

The goal was the Oasis and it was wonderful — a stand of large palm trees and a cool breeze coming down the canyon right through the grove. We closed our eyes, and quieted our minds for a few minutes. In the focus of the gentle breaths and darkness, the oasis came alive with the sounds of birds and insects and water gently bubbling along…you know the idea, the quieter you become, the more you hear!

The time together was excellent. In spite of our age difference (65 and 16 respectively), we found a resonance…an easy rhythm of conversation…you know, the kind that isn't forced…the kind that just happens. Yep, those are the ones I like!

That Virginia family? They arrived at the Oasis about 20 minutes or so after we did…a flush of red faces and by now an empty water bottle, exceedingly grateful for the relatively cool shade the palms afforded. We chatted with them for a few minutes and then headed back to the trailhead. We didn't see them again, but as we finished our hike, we came across a Park Ranger and let her know they were in the canyon, just so someone would keep an eye out for them. We were hoping for them it would not be a "…bad day…"

Time, gravity and my thoughts...

On the drive home, I thought about how the desert is a great metaphor for life itself. On balance, while it can be a wonderful journey, there are a few simple things that can make it a little better. Be prepared for the things you know you will encounter…find people who have been on the trail for a while to get a sense of the kinds of things to look out for. Be sure to arm yourself with the proper 'clothing' (skill set of some kind) to navigate through the challenges that present themselves. Find people with whom you can have those easy and comfortable conversations...build friendships throughout the experiences. Unexpected challenges will occur, and sometimes bad outcomes are unavoidable...those simply are '...not our day...'

At the end of the trail, however, if one has been respectful, the journey can be spectacular!

SPEED MAY NOT KILL, BUT CAN TEACH

"Now, here, you see, it takes all the running
you can do, to keep in the same place.
If you want to get somewhere else, you must
run at least twice as fast as that!"
- The Queen of Hearts: <u>Through the Looking Glass</u>

"Can I go ahead of him?"

She was young and in a hurry…giving off the sense that if she got through faster, her flight would leave earlier. It wasn't that there was really anyone else in the security line at the moment…we were the only two and she wasn't asking me the question.

Learning to fly…
I'm a frequent flyer and have learned one should be ready 'before' getting in the final security line…so I had everything except my bag on the table ready to go through. If there is not a hold up of some kind, I can get my things on the table and the x-ray belt in a little under a minute.

There are two great teachers in the world of frequent flying: Missing a flight because enough time getting to the airport was not allotted, AND miscalculating the length of lines at security checkpoints. Fewer lessons in this world are more dearly learned than missing a flight for one of these reasons!

Be prepared…

There are a few small things concerning traveling, and in particular about the security systems through which we all now pass. Being ready is an enormous stress reliever and requires a little deliberate preparation. It means either having slip on shoes or laces undone ahead of time…it means getting the laptop out of the case and having it in hand before taking the personal item bin…it means putting metal objects, phones, earphones, belts and anything that might set off an alarm, into your laptop bag or carryon <u>prior to getting in line</u>. All of these little things add up to getting into and through security a little…sometimes a lot…less painfully.

Most airports have multiple final lines leading through x-ray and the final visual check. If time is truly a concern, avoid getting in line behind parents with small children or babies. These people tend not to travel much, and as such don't think about what they will have to take off, put away or take out of their baggage in order to get through security. Also, it serves one well to avoid getting behind elderly couples, for often they are a little slower, and sometimes get into brief, and interestingly combative conversations as to which of them is holding the other up in line!

So here we were

It seemed, my young friend must have viewed me as one of those people in the category of elderly. With nary a nod or a yea from the security folk (or me), she jumped ahead, tossed her things on the x-ray belt and prepared to walk through the final check! In fact, she didn't even excuse herself…kind of like I wasn't really there…THE NERVE!!

The next moments were interesting as this young woman revealed herself to be an unseasoned traveler. She moved in front of the sensor gate and received the 'go ahead'. This is where karma and the universe intervened. As she stepped through the alarm went off. It was her belt – by now my things were on the moving through x-ray and I was waiting for her to take off the belt and queue back up to the portal…I waited as she went through a second time only to find the alarm going off again. While she came back out I went through and picked up my things.

By now, she was irritated and a bit chagrined, but for me this was becoming a little entertaining. I had time, so after retrieving all of my things and putting them back where they would remain for my journey, I hung around 'rearranging' my laptop bag.

The girl, it turned out was wearing something in or under her clothing that required a pat down. I didn't want to appear to be a deliberate audience, so I turned my head a little to keep her in my peripheral vision and just listened. Apparently there was some metal wiring in the one of her undergarments setting off the alarm.

From the time this young woman got into line behind me – for what should have been no longer than a 30 to 45 second pass through – 10 minutes expired and seven or eight additional people arrived and moved through the line.

Ah the universe, you've got to love it. The only thing that tempered a mild sense of satisfaction was the memory of any number of times in my life where impatience bred inattention…which led to repeating a task when it wasn't necessary. You know the sayings, "There's never enough time to do it right the first time but always enough time to do it over," or "…measure twice cut once…"

While I had a quiet smile about the incident and the number of times I had been in her place, I wondered if it was a teaching moment for her. Glancing at her face, during the pat down, there seemed a combination of anger and maybe a little humiliation. I did not get the sense she saw this as anything other than a royal inconvenience…surely not a broader teaching moment.

Two ships passing…
The girl was not on my flight, so I never saw her again, but was reminded that no matter the circumstances, we only have control over the thoughts about them. Disrespected or entertained? That is pretty much what it came down to.

During the times in my life when I have had (been provided?) uncomfortable and sometimes embarrassing 'teaching moments,' –

there have been many – I am clear about one thing. They did not seem educational...it could be argued I needed an over abundance of them to yield the benefit...you know, practice, practice, practice. In was nice to see this situation as entertainment and not offense. It was one of those moments reminding me I am grateful for the small lessons I have actually learned.

The rest of my journey went exceedingly well...I hope hers did too.

RUGBY, SCHOOL KIDS, MEANING

"If we are to go forward, we must go back
and rediscover those precious values -
that... [hinge] on moral foundations..."
- Martin Luther King

"Ladies and gentlemen, I give you the pride of our nation, winners of the Rugby World Cup...The New Zealand All Blacks!!!"

The words of the Mayor of Wellington as the team arrived for post victory celebrations.

These men, all-stars from provincial leagues all over the country, had won the cup by one point. It could not have been sweeter, for not only did the All Blacks win for New Zealand; they did it in Wellington with the eyes of the world focused on them.

The tradition, so hard to explain to those unfamiliar with the game, the work, the dedication, the focus, the values...all of them came together that day for 4 million New Zealanders needing every bit of this tradition for their country.

Earlier that day
"Are these your children working behind the counter?" I asked. "Yes," she said, "They are here in the morning and then go off to school"

There were three youngsters – two girls, one boy – and two adult women. It was a small breakfast shop just off the harbor, on Victoria Street. I was hungry from having walked for an hour and a half along the shore in the chilly and blustery morning air. One of the young girls, dressed in her school uniform, had just taken my order and disappeared into the kitchen.

Coming to town...

I had arrived there the day before and taken a shuttle to the hotel from the airport. It happened to be at the afternoon school break and children were on their way home in streams and small groups – all wearing uniforms. At first I thought they were from a private school – most of the boys in light blue shirts, navy shorts with knee socks and black shoes...some in long trousers...many more shorts than trousers on this overcast and windy afternoon. The girls were in similar tops and matching tartan skirts. Some, both boys and girls, wearing sweaters against the afternoon chill.

Continuing to the city, I passed two or three other schools, with boys and girls dressed in similar style, but different colors. These were NOT private schools, but simply traditional colors representing the children's institutions – for the most part, I later learned, worn proudly.

The morning had been good so far...the walk, a warm breakfast and a small window into New Zealand culture. The girl serving me in the restaurant, by her uniform had a tangible sense of connection to her school, AND was getting a family/business 'life lesson' in the importance of responsibility and discipline.

Right place right time...

I had not planned to be here for the celebrations, in truth, I didn't even know the World Cup was on, or that it was being held in Wellington. It was France the All Blacks beat by a point on the weekend, and by all accounts, nobody in the country breathed during the last 10 minutes. The team was here to celebrate their victory with the people from whom they themselves had come. In a country with a population of 4 million, this was not just a big deal...it was an indescribable and intimate moment for both groups. These men weren't just a professional team who had provided this small Island country bragging rights...they were family and you could feel it...all these boys known by the people.

School was cancelled for the afternoon and more than one hundred thousand Kiwis filled the streets and the Parliament grounds where the parade would end – one in three Wellingtonians attended this event.

I slipped into the City Center Square with several thousand other folk to see the beginning of the festivities. When the All Blacks arrived the people exploded into a bedlam of joy…a truly unbridled mass of humanity, in that moment, *one* with each other…for there is no sport in New Zealand so universally popular as Rugby.

The Mayor of Wellington spoke a few words saying how the team had not only made New Zealand proud of their success, but injected a much needed boost of energy and hope into a City and country that had recently seen the Christ Church earthquake, a large oil spill and hard economic times. None of that seemed to matter on this day.

School children – Rugby…all of us

The All Blacks...a team…yet more – a tradition around which people gathered - embracing the moment and believing with hope, the boys would be able to repeat again next year. Satisfied in the moment, but also something to look forward to. To find meaning in life, no matter the medium, looking forward seems to be key. Whether we recognize it or not, we hunger for something to look forward to.

Traditions provide ways to look forward. Some occur at yearly intervals such as religious, political, athletic or social holidays. Others a little more subtle...the institution of marriage, for example, as we seek the stability of a mate. Even more subtle things such as working daily before school…constancy, expectation with familiarity, things that seem known to us…a way to fit in and feel a part. These are the things that provide anchors for our lives.

Traditions are important, often acting as bridges to meaning. That is not to say traditions necessarily bring meaning…but they bring structure. Repeating 'the known' helps create value systems of loyalty… commitment… dependability… honesty.

Values are what give life meaning. Circumstances change, jobs change, uniforms change, team loyalties change, but values that are learned through repetitive events in our lives, seldom do. We learn the core of these when we are children, and they follow us for our whole lives.

Both ends met

On this chilly day in Wellington, I had the opportunity to see both the early stages of value creation and an end result. Both had uniforms identifying what they did or where they were educated

The young girl at the breakfast shop, dressed in *her* school uniform, doing routine work before school, building traditions and creating values of dedication and discipline in her life.

The 'All Blacks' in their uniforms, winning a championship because of the values of dedication, discipline, hard work, team effort...values they had learned as youngsters when they were growing up.

On the measuring line of life, these values being learned as a youth and exercised as an adult provide a sense of meaning to our lives.

On this chilly and rainy day in Wellington, I was pleased to have had the opportunity to see some in the early process and others a little further along, sharing some common values that gave meaning to their lives.

Oh yes, and reminding me, as I see the sun begin to move gently closer toward the distant horizon of life, how values become more than simply ideas we live by...they become close and intimate friends.

EVERY OTHER BOOK

I'm afraid of taking steps that are not on the map,
but by taking those steps despite my fears,
I have a much more interesting life.
- Paulo Coelho

Lisa and I had known each other for quite a few years. We met when I was in graduate school. Subsequent to that, we joined the same church and saw each other several times a week for nearly three decades. We played in the church band together – she a piano player...me rhythm guitar player – rhythm guitar...a euphemism for mediocre play.

"I thought you might enjoy this book," she said handing me a copy of Colin Powell's autobiography. I smiled and said with little attempt to hide the shallowness of my intellectual curiosity, "I really don't read non-fiction. You know, the ending is not a surprise."

"Well," she continued undaunted as though I had said nothing, "I think you would like it anyway." With a faint smile I took the book, knowing because I saw her regularly, I would be reading this book!

I have enjoyed reading most of my life, but up until then, spent most of my time in fiction. Outside of the scripture and my professional reading, I had greatly enjoyed Michael Connolly, Pat Conroy, Lee Childs, Danial Silva, and Ken Follett, among a fair number of other writers. Mysteries and broad-brush stories of life, heroic battles against all odds, and love drew my attention.

Lisa's recommendation turned out to be a surprisingly good, and much more entertaining read than I had anticipated. Reading this book actually altered my life. To be fair, it wasn't exactly the book. It was the decision following the book that changed everything.

A tiny course change...

Powell's book seemed enjoyable enough that I thought, "What if every other book I read for the next year is one I wouldn't read under any circumstance?" For surely, left to my own devices, I would not have read this one. I'm not exactly sure how the idea emerged, but I figured with the demands of life, one year of alternating books like this couldn't be that painful!

At first this new rhythm was awkward. The initial book was the Lord Russell's, <u>The Trial of Adolf Eichmann</u>, probably not the best first pick for length, but as it turned out, it was a real page-turner. How Eichmann was eventually tracked down and captured in Brazil was as good as any spy novel I had read. My incentive, however, was to get through the book so I could reward myself with my normal fare.

That first year went by out of shear discipline and duty. I haven't always kept my resolutions, but for some reason I slogged through the tall grass for the next 12 months.

As the year ended, the friction of reading new things didn't seem so bad, and I had, in fact, actually enjoyed a couple of the books. I thought, maybe I would see if I could do it for another year.

Year two...

During the '...second year of planting...' an interesting thing began to happen. I found myself pushing my way through the novels a little more quickly, in anticipation of the landscape of the '...next unknown...' world to be revealed. The criterion for choosing each book was simple. I would wander over to the nonfiction section of the library and glance at the titles, thinking to myself, "Who would read this kind of book?" This would become the next choice! Over time, I found that more and more I was standing in front of history and philosophy sections, with a biography or two along the way.

71

Small course corrections...

In the years since that small decision, everything has changed about the way I read and the things I am interested in. Over that time, I have been unable to finish only three or four books I had chosen. The first unfinished title was Amy Tan's The Bonesetter's Daughter. I picked it from a best seller's list, and gave it a pretty heroic effort, but some 200 pages in; I just could not bring myself to read any more. I found the same thing in Fitzgerald's The Great Gatsby, and Oscar Wilde's "The Picture of Dorian Gray. I felt badly that I couldn't 'get them,' but I just didn't have what it took to finish them up...failure with Gatsby a particular disappointment, because it is considered an American classic by one of this country's most celebrated writers.

Over the years nothing is the same. New, and formerly completely unknown, worlds have opened up. I have found 'friends' from bygone eras who expressed thoughts and feelings I had, but could not put into words. I have traveled the seas, poked through jungles, and felt the fears as well as joys of men and women able to paint canvases in brilliant and subtle shades of color. I have found the kinds of writers that resonate with my soul like the harmonics of a cosmic harp in the universe, that when plucked, vibrate and touch my heart as if the author were in the room whispering intimately in my ear.

I have come to appreciate that most everything I thought to be unique has happened again and again and again and again. The intrigue, the political debate and vilification of one's opponent, the love, the fidelity, the betrayal – whether today or in Empires past...it's all the same.

Solomon was right, "The thing that hath been, it is that which shall be; and that which is done is that which shall be done: and there is no new thing under the sun." (Ecclesiastes 1:9).

I have, however, come to appreciate that purchasing tickets to become a 'peeping Tom' into the minds of thoughtful people has expanded almost everything about the way I think, and that, maybe with foresight, minimize the mistakes of the past in the going forward.

I would like to be able to say, this part of my life's journey was the result of a deliberate effort to increase the quality of my life. I would like to say that I had a burning and unquenchable intellectual curiosity. I would like to say that I am insightful and take the broader view of things. All of that, of course, would be utter nonsense! My life perceptions changed because I didn't want to disappoint my friend Lisa…it was by accident, and I might add, in retrospect, a happy accident indeed.

Wrapping around the edges…

In the end, it's the one degree of change that makes the difference. You know how the story goes…two boats begin a journey together, bows pointed just one-degree different. In the early going, it appears they are heading in the same direction, but over time, they drift further and further apart until eventually, they are completely out of sight from one another. It was a one-degree of difference of direction in my life by adding to what I was reading, that completely altered the trajectory of thought…the apparent original destination completely out of sight. This small course shift, at the moment, seemed to be nothing more than a minor adjustment in my peripheral vision.

I haven't seen Lisa for quite some time. Life and circumstance has changed all of that. However, every time I pick up another spyglass that allows me to peek into the mind of those men and women who have labored to share their thoughts and ideas with me, I think of her.

The next time you find yourself looking for a good read, why not try something YOU would never read under any circumstance…you might be pleasantly surprised!

COMING HOME

"No one realizes how beautiful it is to travel until he comes
home and rests his head on his old, familiar pillow."
- Lyn Yutang

Hotels are pretty much the same. You know what I'm talking
about — a little stale...depending on the price, maybe a little air
freshener, but above all — sterile!

It really doesn't matter much once the lights are out. It is usually
about the bed...maybe the desk...maybe the Internet...yeah, the
Internet.

The week had been busy, and at week's end there was that trip to
Chicago. The flight scheduled for Thursday...but something was
wrong. You know...that nagging undercurrent that some balance has
shifted...a change has occurred. The email on Friday confirmed it.

A few days earlier...
There was another week in another part of the country that had
also gotten under way, with another fellow preparing for a trip. It had
been a hard week — you know the kind. It had followed a hard week
before and one before that. When weeks and months have been
difficult, the exhaustion becomes almost routine...the sense of
fatigue so bone penetrating that there appears to be no hope.

This fellow's trip had been a long time coming and he deserved
it...it had been earned the old-fashioned way...hard work, integrity,
virtue, honesty...all of the things that when exercised on a regular

basis form character. Character?? His life defined it!

In many ways both of these men were looking forward to their flight. Neither would need to pack a lot…there wasn't much required at the other end. One was leaving home…the other going home.

Both trips had itineraries…a sense of meaning, but in the end, one meant more.

That is the thing about going out and coming home, isn't it? The excitement of a new place…a new adventure…the experiences yet unknown…the place untested. When the journey has been completed, it is time to come home…for the traveler, there is little better than coming home…

It's hard to know how or why…
The thing about these two men is that they were friends. One a little older than the other – he reached out first. The older fellow was Jim Priester…the younger me, and it had begun with a phone call in the fall of 1964, coming after a heart breaking weekend loss to our chief rival football team on a sunny Saturday afternoon.

"Hi Ted, this is Coach Priester (the rival team)." "I heard Coach Feltz. (my team) didn't get that touchdown on film. We got it and I thought you might like to see it."

Just as the first half of the football game ended, I had caught one of those long, long passes – the kind every kid dreams about – and scored a touchdown. The film from our cameras had run out Just before the play. The rival's had not! The next evening I was in Priester's home eating a little pizza and watching that film!

Who was this man??

There was something about Jim that struck my heart like a marksman's bullet…straight and true. He had singled me out…made me feel special. I thought it was me, but in fact it was him. I had simply found myself 'in the sights' of his gift…his calling – the cultivation and guidance of young men. In fact, as it turns out, I was only one of uncounted numbers of young men who were influenced by this man. I've known many gifted motivators in my time...Jim was the best of them all.

This small gesture began a relationship that would continue for decades. There weren't long hours spent together – really not much in the way of quantity at all. It was just that in the most critical of moments, when important course corrections were needed, this man emerged.

There would be no way to know at the time how significant this man would be in my life, nor would there be time or space now to write about how his influence rippled through the decades. In those days, his gift seemed to be always 'at the ready.' It was smooth, practiced, direct, always seeming to know exactly what was needed. Each time, his encouragement was significant, and in the end it altered the course of my life.

Oh yeah, the flight...
The attendants on my flight were friendly and pleasant – that's really their business, you know. They greeted me with a smile and welcomed me aboard. They pointed me down the aisle toward my seat. I took my place, fastened the seatbelt and waited for the flight to take off.

Jim's flight had a little more personal touch. He was tired as he made his way down the entryway. As he stepped on board, it wasn't the flight attendant that greeted him...it was the captain. It was a warm greeting as the pilot gathered Jim in his arms and held him closely for <u>his</u> flight home. This would be the last flight from this dimension of time and space...he would be landing in a different place.

The email was short and direct...
I had been in meetings all day and it was dark outside when I turned on the computer and saw the message in the 'in-box.' It had been there from the morning.

"Ted - Thought you would want to know – Stan"

I read the accompanying obituary, and turned off the lights in my room. In the quiet darkness of that place, the image of his gentle face slipped softly into my mind and I wept. I wept for the family he left behind, who had loved him so deeply, and who had carried the burden of his care in recent years...I wept for all those whose lives had been touched by him...I wept for his courage and faith...the nagging undercurrent the past couple of days had been correct – the balance had shifted...I wept for me.

Over the years, I have studied and accumulated the language of faith. I know the words and have used them many times myself...but what do I really know?

I know this...in the sorrow and pain of loss, there is freedom...in the desperate desire to understand, there is faith...in the despair of the empty heart, there is love.

You may never have known this man, but I am certain there is a 'Jim Priester' somewhere in your life...along your journey. I am certain God has a way of putting these people on our paths...to be there when we "...hunger and thirst..." And so in this time of loss I also rejoice for the honor of having known and walked part of my life's pathway with this generous and thoughtful soul...

It has been said, we are the accumulation of all those we have known in our lives...some hold more space than others. In the quality of my life, he held much...

THREE CATS AND THE SETTING SUN

"Big wheel keeps on turnin',
Proud Mary keeps on burnin'…"
- John Fogerty

It was a little after seven pm…you know the time…those special moments when the sun slips into the horizon bringing with it dusk like the tail of a cosmic python pulling itself West…I mean where does the tail really begin and end? Wisps of clouds remaining in the sky turned from white, to bright red, to light pink and then grayish specters in the approaching evening sky.

The four of us were sitting in the small back yard making up the area behind each home in the 1950s 'legacy' neighborhood in which we live. "Legacy" meaning '…these houses have been here for 50 years or so, and most of the people living in them are related to the original owners.

Our little home faces south, so when I sit on the small concrete slab that slips out into our backyard like the deck of a moderate sized swimming pool, I am pointed north. That means as the light imperceptibly slips away to the horizon on my left, the sky to my right slowly deepens its shade from blue to gray in perfect harmony with the changing colors of the clouds. The evening melody becomes muted…a thoughtful transition to a 'minor key…'

Cats are different…
The girls and I have odd relationships – each in a quite different way. While I know they love, er…like, ah…tolerate me, it is only

occasionally we find comfort in communal proximity – for the most part, they are Molly's cats.

Sitting in the backyard as dusk arrives '...stage right...' is one of those times. For an unknown reason, that I am confident even t.s. Elliot, to the music of Andrew Lloyd Weber's CATS, would not understand. They arrived silently, each taking a post not far from my chair - their collective presence an enigma to me.

Leah has been my early morning and late night companion for a good part of the 12 years of her life. In recent months, maybe because of the development of a slowly encroaching arthritic spine, she has been a little less loving on the edges of the day. Oh, she still comes to wake me with a purring engine even the neighbors could hear, but she seems less inclined to lie on my tummy as much. In fact, I miss that when it doesn't happen.

Sarah has made it a mission to conscientiously ignore and/or disrespect me. If she is on the bed when I slip in, she turns her head away or gives me the "...excuse me, do you still live here?? look..." before leaping away with disgust. If I walk in a room where she is, I get '...the look...' and off she trots; if I am making my way down the hall, she makes sure I walk around her before continuing on her way. Anyone who thinks cats don't have facial expressions, clearly does not own a Sarah!

Hannah is the largest, by far, of our feline family. She is the whiner, and talker. Often it seems she chatters simply to hear her own voice. In spite of being the biggest of the girls, she is the most skittish. She is one of those cats that seems to be in a constant state of agitation. She will sit beside you on the couch... then to the shallow rectangular box on the floor by the bookcase...then to the door asking to go out. She appears full of nervous glances checking the room to see what dangers might be lurking just around the corner.

A little darker...
The backyard was now slipping into that special time when the sharp edges of the trees, bird feeder and cactus begin to soften...that

magic time when sounds of the day become quiet and the evening critters tune their instruments looking for dinner and the possibility of an insect date or two.

This is also the time when imagination begins to exert its special pull. It is easy to see the yard becoming a mysterious and secret world...a place that can be anything I want it to be...a time when I can clear my mind and slip into the soft and isolated darkness...I like that.

The cats also seem to change as their senses sharpen in the nightfall. Our little yard becomes a primal hunting ground. They sit, crouch and listen, occasionally moving across the grass, like 'big cat' ancestors on the expansive savannahs of the African or Indian continents. They become the hunters! To me this is entertaining...to them deadly serious.

This evening, a neighborhood stray made the mistake of mounting the fence in the back northeast corner of the yard. As darkness increased, pushing away the fading light of day, Hannah suddenly went on alert. Gone her apparent insecurities as her muscles tightened, tail doubled in size, her eyes set in deliberate focus. With the stealth of a python slithering through the grass, she advanced on her prey...a few steps and pause – frozen in space...the cycle repeated several times. Watching a domesticated cat on the prowl is kind of awesome. The whiney timid cat evaporated with a low growl and quiet hiss, like a drop of water at high noon on a hot rock, in the Arizona desert ...as Leah, Sarah and I watched, the lioness approached her prey!

Just as she disappeared into the melting dusk of fading and colorless light, she pounced! There was a brief tussle, a fair amount of growling, indistinct screeching noises, and then silence. While I couldn't quite see into the darkened corner of the yard, she reemerged, trotting back to where we were sitting to reassure us the yard was once again safe.

It was darker now, just a hint to pinkish light at the base of the horizon in the western sky. As the cosmic dial continued to turn, another light began to slowly appear. As I stared upward, I saw one star, then a few – eventually the black sky filled with twinkling lights...too many to count. They came quietly, without fanfare and caused me to wonder once again about the magnitude of life...how our minds could at once consider both the micro and macro things of the universe, how this happens every single day, and yet is uniquely different each time.

The day was done...

These are the moments I relish and make me glad that I am alive...when I at once feel both a part of the living universe and at the same time utterly insignificant. I was reminded of David's words in the Psalms "...what is man that thou art mindful of him..." Who <u>are</u> we and why are we so privileged in this way?

When I slow my mind down and let it get quiet, I know with certainty there is more to life than meets the eye...there is something that God gives...to see the world for what it is – or at least 'what it is to each of us.'

LISTEN TO THIS

"Reason is the slow and tortuous method by
which those who do not know
the truth discover it."
- B. Pascal: <u>Pensées</u>

The coach yells, "Throw the ball!" – the teacher says, "If you divide the number ten by two, the answer is five." – The lover whispers, "You mean more to me than life itself..." Each of these messages carries an idea, meaning and most surprising of all, feeling.

No big deal you say??

The system – in general terms...
The grunting sounds to the untrained ear are just that – nondescript noises. Sometimes they come with greater or lesser intensity.... sometimes at faster – sometimes slower rates. You've seen the cartoon of two people chatting in the presence of a cat. One gal says to the other, "How do you think the elections will go this year?" The cat hears, "Blah, blah, blah, blah...."

The vibrations originate in the vocal cords, are pushed out by the lungs with the expiration of air, and amplified by an echo chamber – the mouth. Whatever the characteristic of the sounds; whatever the rhythm or musicality, the noises have meaning...when and only when, a receptor has been trained to receive them.

Emerging sounds come through a monophonic megaphone, and are best received when the noisemaker is pointed in the direction of the intended receiver. The receivers, in this case, are small stereophonic microphones attached to the sides of our heads with cartilaginous sound collectors channeling the clatter into the ear canals like whitewater tumbling down the Colorado River. If the noise is not directed precisely at the receivers, these 'sound catchers' work in just enough asynchrony to help discern the direction from which the sound is coming.

How it works – in general terms...

The unseen noises, carried by pulses of vibrating air, work a little like this. Energetic invisible grunts hit the eardrum like fingers tapping the surface of a bongo drum. The intensity and specific rhythm of those thumps cause three little bones on the other side of the 'drum head' to vibrate. The last of these oscillating bones strikes a little snail shaped organ filled with fluid and little hairs – each tuned to a specific frequency from 20 cycles to 20,000 cycles per second.

The vibrating fluid creates small waves that stimulate the little hairs, leading to tiny micro-electric currents that travel through organic wiring (neurons) to the decoding portion of the brain and VOILA the sound moving through space – no wires folks – has created an idea in our minds!!

Take a moment – this is very cool...

No one reading this needs to understand the system to use it, although it took centuries of study to comprehend it. In fact it is such a routine part of life, we give it no thought at all...and yet, not only is it arguably the most important mechanical and physiological system for the communal human experience...it is even more fundamentally amazing than that.

Speaking and hearing communicate ideas, but more remarkably, this system transmits feelings: the passion of joy and sorrow, the expression of enthusiasm or caution, the transmission of love and faith...the intangibles.

On balance, within relatively narrow parameters, we create these noises, and in the most incredible of ways, others receive and make some sort of sense out of them...at least enough sense for collective communication and survival.

Before the advent of all of the technology by which we live our lives, this system of communication, in its most basic form, was the foundation for the rise and fall of empires...peace or war amongst peoples...the passing along of tradition...the ways in which we found common ground...one of the most fundamentally profound reasons we survive. If the system were just understandable bursts of noise that transmitted ideas, it would be impressive, BUT this...this is miraculous!

It is easy to take for granted the normal day-to-day automatic systems by which we live our lives. They permit us to look for things out of the ordinary...new ideas...new movies...new books...in general, the news by which we live our lives.

A small point to be made...
The origin of speech, transmission of thought or understanding from seemingly indistinct noises, is not the focus here. The point is that so much of what comes with the normality of the lives we live is awesome and honestly, if given thought, overwhelming!

Our breath, the beating of our hearts, the muscular engines of movement, the internal factories that process the energy we consume, and yes the way we communicate...all of it is stunning in the way it runs quietly in the background while we get on with our days. Unless something gets out of place, unless we suffer from some disruption of the system...some dis-ease...we ignore these background, life giving systems.

The next time you hear the coach yell, a teacher teach or the love of your life whisper something intimate in your ear, remember what an amazing and unsolicited communication system we have been given...

Looking for a miracle? Perk up your ears...you are living in one!

PASSING THE BATON

"Realization may come at the speed of light,
Clarity? It comes at the speed of dark…"
- anonymous

It was early in the day. She stood at the window, as she did every morning, in every season, staring at Lake Ontario. The hot tea in her cup, only slightly sipped, cooling on the windowsill to in front of her. She could easily have been a sentry on early morning watch, straining at the horizon for any movement, any clue to impending danger.

She wasn't, of course, she was simply Martha Jackson, preparing for the day as she did with clocklike precision every morning…No, she was more than that, she was my grandmother – "Nana" – an austere and mysterious woman, built like a Slavic factory worker, as combative as a human being could be…and as gentle as a lioness tenderly watching over her pride.

It was the time of day when she gathered herself…the time of day she considered what she expected was coming…the time of day she would humbly ask God to forgive her for the sins of days gone by. No priestly confession…she was, after all, a Protestant. Her confessor the Almighty, and as she knew in her heart – like the rest of the world – the list was long.

This, of course, was a mystery to me. All I saw was the woman staring out the widow, apparently catatonic…an almost palpable bubble surrounding her…in its silence loudly proclaiming: DO NOT

DISTURB!

I never saw her at the beginning of this morning routine…5AM, in those days, seemed unnatural. The summer I lived with her and got ready for work, I would catch her toward the 6 O'clock hour as she 'returned' from the window from whence she had begun her early morning journey…her face and spirit serene.

I didn't understand why she did this, I mean, what was there to see? The best I could tell, there appeared to be nothing!

A powerful memory…
It's hard not to think about her, from time to time, sitting in the cool morning air…coffee cup still warm in my hand. If it weren't such a good time to prepare for the day, the coffee would still be hot as I finished it, but this is the quiet time, the time before the day begins…the time for rebirth…the coffee seems to have instantly chilled as I slip away for 'just a moment…just a moment.'

While Martha Jackson was and remains a bigger than life enigma to me, the early morning ritual seems to have been passed on through her genetic code to me. I am uncertain what she saw, but when returning from these moments, there is a serenity that I covet.

Faith was important…
What I came to understand later in my life is that my grandmother was simply stepping into her closet to pray. She was a religious woman, somewhat of a paradox considering her often hard exterior, but she believed the scriptures and did her best to follow them. She knew she had things to work on, and her discipline of reading the scriptures, helped keep her centered. God only knows what she would have been like, had she not taken those mornings to reflect!

There are so many self-help books in the market place, with lists and lists of things to do intended to make our lives better, yet we often overlook the simplicity of the scripture's gentle reminder:

"But thou, when thou prayest, enter into thy closet, and when thou hast shut thy door, pray to thy Father which is in secret; and thy

Father which seeth in secret shall reward thee openly."

"After this manner therefore pray ye: Our Father which art in heaven, Hallowed be thy name. Thy kingdom come, Thy will be done in earth, as it is in heaven.
Give us this day our daily bread.
And forgive us our debts, as we forgive our debtors.
And lead us not into temptation, but deliver us from evil: For thine is the kingdom, and the power, and the glory, forever. Amen"
Matthew 6:6, 10-13 – Bible

These words in Matthew are powerful in their quiet simplicity. Close the door of our minds from the hubbub of the surrounding chaotic world...quietly center ourselves...recognize the magnitude of the intelligent creative universe we call God...be grateful for the sacred human fabric of which we are all a part. Remind ourselves to be diligent...to 'eat the bread' of knowledge and understanding...to help us avoid the pitfalls in life that so easily rob us of our dignity and brotherhood...to recognize we are indeed part of an extraordinary universe, where we have the ability to appreciate both God, and its magnitude. "Amen – so be it!"

Who knows, other than blind obedience to her faith, what led my grandmother to practice this morning ritual. Who knows at what point the practice turned from duty to habit and from habit to the constitution of her being. Yet part of the absolute tapestry of her life it became. At some point it was no longer, "I need to do this" or "I want to do this." It became "This is who I am."

Like grandmother, like grandson...
While I don't really have any idea what my grandmother was thinking in those early morning hours, I know this...the example of her dedication caught my attention, and dropped a pebble into the liquid chemistry of my mind. It took some time before those concentric ripples made their way to the shores of conscious thought for me, but arrive they did, and here I sit.

This is the time of day when I gather myself, the time of day I consider what I expect is coming, the time of day I ask God to forgive me for the sins of the days gone by. No priestly confession…I am, after all, a Protestant. My confessor the Almighty, and I know in my heart the list is long.

EVERY DAY BEGINS AGAIN

"Begin at the beginning and go on till
you come to the end: then stop."
King to the White Rabbit
Carrol, L. Alice's Adventures in Wonderland

It's all about communication isn't it? Finding ways to share our world…the world (mind) in which we live, with the worlds of others. Communication is the basis for expressing and receiving meaning in life.

Think about the alphabet. It starts with the letter 'a' and ends 25 letters later with 'z'. Twenty-six individual letters building words…then sentences and paragraphs, leading to essays, stories and books, allowing us to communicate by the written word.

It is awe-inspiring to consider the sheer volume of written material based on these simple, seemingly meaningless letters. Yet through the mixing and matching of them, commerce has developed, countries formed, hearts made to soar and minds to imagine the unimaginable.

For the teller of tales, there is the drive to express ideas, convey stories and communicate impressions. The reader becomes, in a sense, the voyeur who peeks into the story as well as the mind (world) of the author.

Nothing written…
There was a time when all that existed was in oral tradition. The

spoken word carried the message to the ear of the hearer. Stories of the valiant fell from the lips of the gifted tellers, to the ears of the fortunate who heard them. These were passed from mind to mind, generation to generation, taking on new life, and enrichment as they traveled through the years. Some say oral traditions have existed for 50 to 100 thousand years!

Around 6 thousand years ago, an area known as the Fertile Crescent in the region of the Tigris and Euphrates Rivers, (general area of Iraq today), pictures began to emerge...orderly pictures – or pictographs – that could be used consistently to express ideas without the presence of the 'teller of the tale.' From these formative efforts, came written language(s).

Written language, constructed of sentences, typically have a subject (noun) and some action identifying something the subject does. Life is a little bit like this.

The sentence of life...

Each of us is a story of sorts, made up of a spiritual alphabet – for lack of a better term. In the mixing pot of life, we all have a similar foundation from which we emerge. Like letters of the alphabet, we are made up of basic elements such as wisdom, peace, understanding, faith, curiosity, joy, anger, gentleness, envy, greed, and this list goes on.

To carry the metaphor... life is composed of nouns and verbs. We, the life force/soul are the central focus in the sentence of our lives – the noun. That, of course is not enough, for there must be a verb, an action. Without action, there is not much life - life rewards action.

The unique mixing and matching of these characteristic components create the distinctive individual we are. It is awe-inspiring to see the innumerable mixtures of personalities that emerge through the 'spiritual alphabet' from which we are created.

What is the story?

We then become the teller of the tale – the tale of our lives. We tell it every time we meet or interact with someone. Recognizing and understanding we have control over the sentences we write with our lives, the clearer and more focused our lives become.

Cultivating curiosity will make it stronger, exercising understanding will cause it to grow, nurturing kindness will make it excel.

Occupying and focusing our life journey on writing a positive novel has other benefits…starve anger and it will dissipate; re-channel frustration and watch it whither; change focus from our envy and watch it dissolve. This doesn't mean pretending these characteristics are not there, but actively choosing to engage something else in their place is the key. Following our heart and passion will determine the outcome, plain and simple. For better or worse, we become what we exercise in our lives. It is in our control.

Choose this day!

We are all authors and storytellers. The complete story of our lives is yet untold, every minute of every day we have the opportunity to choose the things we want to write in our book of life. What has been written in the past, may inform the present, but absolutely DOES NOT have to predict what the next event will be. The next chapter will be determined by the choices we make right now, at this moment in time.

Setting a plan regarding the way we want to live in our world (mind), is up to us and nobody else. We do not have to simply be a bystander and or a victim of our thoughts and feelings.

Pick up a notebook and sketch out where you would like to be, and don't be surprised at the adventure when you find yourself there.

DOORS AND STORES

"Resolve to be thyself: and know, that he
who finds himself, loses his misery."
- Matthew Arnold

I was sitting in the coffee shop waiting for Bill. We meet early Wednesday mornings to chat about...well, whatever is on the burner for the week. We don't talk much about the hot button items of the day – you know, the politics, the movies, the sex, the sports...it is mostly just two older fellas who have found some mutual pathways - exploring the resonance...the small personal and spiritual stuff. The sort of things friends do...nothing special...you know what I mean...like a pair of old tennis shoes – quietly comfortable.

We typically meet pretty early, but occasionally get our schedules mixed up. We are usually good about communicating, but this was one of those mornings when we had not checked in the day before, and he was a no show – I've missed our meetings a time or two as well.

A wandering mind...

You know how it is when you have a few minutes, waiting to get something started...there really isn't time to work on anything in particular, or to get into a focused train of thought...you are just waiting. While sitting there, a song from the 1960s slipped out of my memory banks and drifted across my consciousness... "It never rains in Southern California." The title is ironic because the chorus actually goes:

"...It never rains in California – But girl don't they warn ya – It

92

pours, man it pours…"

Like the lyrics of that iconic Albert Hammond song from a bygone era, it was raining this particular morning and raining hard!

Wants and needs…

The music playing in the coffee shop was Vivaldi – surely different from the 60s rock song in my head. I was looking out the window in front of me, with the unfocused gaze of a camera lens poorly adjusted. Just to the front was a small, open-air walkway running between the coffee place and some shops across the way. A small, flower-decorated pond with a fountain, sat in the middle of the path where shoppers could easily move from store to store lining the walkway. These kinds of little stores are common in the Mediterranean climate Southern California is so famous for, because, in fact rain really doesn't very often come.

Since it was early, it would be several hours before these stores opened. As I looked through the pouring rain, across the open walkway, I wondered, "If all the doors, of all the stores were open, AND I could take whatever I wanted, what would I take?" How much would I take? When would it be enough?

I thought about that for a few moments, working through my list if items. While this exercise was taking place, a second thought popped into my mind with a bit of a twist.

"If all the doors, of all the stores were open, AND I could take whatever I needed, what would I take?" How much of what I needed would I take? When would that be enough?

Wants vs. Needs…an old dilemma in the story of human nature. What is the measure by, or context through which one makes the decision?

Some things to ponder…

It's all really relative, isn't? For example, if you live in a first world country, have a decent job and gotten used to a particular lifestyle, you might take certain things based on the questions above – the potential for gathering practically limitless.

If you were, as is half the world's population, living on less than $2.00US per day, with little more than your clothing, some shelter and hard won food for the day, you might have a totally different 'want to need' ratio in your life...and you probably would not be reading this.

There is something about '...not having...' with barriers '...to getting...', that makes '...wanting to have...' take center stage in our minds. This sometimes leads us to gather things we may have little use for....keeping them on hand, you now...just in case. It is surprising how much time we spend occupying our minds with the wanting and the getting. Much of this is tied to how we value ourselves, or more importantly how we think others value us. In fact, this is nothing more than background noise in our lives.

It's all a metaphor

Feeling we want and need things, is really a reflection of a much deeper want and a more thoughtful need. Thinking about these questions led me to a series of ideas regarding spiritual pathways and spiritual stores, and the things we want and need out of life. Not clothing or jewelry or computers or the latest phone technology, but rather wisdom or faith or understanding or joy or happiness – not just the pursuit of happiness...things for which we have the most primal of desires. The things we get at the literal store satisfy us for the briefest of time. The things we get from the spiritual stores of life are more difficult to attain, but infinitely more satisfying.

Is there a point here?

The conversation in life is not about the big things, the mountains yet to climb, the drive to have things that proclaim we are something or somebody. Rather, it is a conversation that feels comfortable like an old pair of tennis shoes. It is about finding an internal resonance, a quiet dialogue between friends. At this time in life, there is a realization that my best friend should be me – the creature that lives inside the body I inhabit, the friend who carries the name "Ted." As my journey has become a little longer on the planet, THIS is what I

WANT…more importantly THIS is what I NEED.

Time and gravity have caused my 'want to need' ratio to become much more aligned…isn't this the way it should be?

IT'S GOOD TO COME HOME

"Homeward bound, I wish I was homeward bound
Home, where my thoughts escapin',
home, where my music's playin'
Home, where my love lies waitin'
silently for me."
- Paul Simon

Sometimes you have the opportunity to catch your breath…take a look around and settle into a comforting thought or two. Life can be so busy with things occupying our time that we don't have moments to reflect.

Reflection [ri flékshan]:
 The act of reflecting or the state of being reflected.
 An image; representation; counterpart.
 Fixing of the thoughts on something; careful consideration.
 A thought occurring in consideration or meditation.

Outward bound…
When I was younger, I looked forward to traveling. I can remember the first time I journeyed overseas. Well, the first time was to Vietnam and that time was so hectic and full of things to do, from a military standpoint, it is a bit of a blur. No, the first time would come many years later, 26 years to be precise, when I had an opportunity to speak in Würzburg, Germany.

I remember sitting in a small circle of researchers in the Marriot Hotel in La Jolla, California. We had just finished a spine conference and a few of the faculty were reviewing the conference. A couple of Swiss folks were going to put on a conference in Wüzburg the following year and asked whether I might be interested in speaking. I said casually, "I think I can do this. I'll check my calendar to confirm the dates."

That's what I said. My thoughts were quite different…"Are you kidding me?? You want me to do what??? Europe?? Pay me??" In truth, the excitement was so extreme I had to clasp my hands together to keep them from shaking with enthusiasm!

Well prepped…

As a youngster, my mother provided the guiding light for my life. During the day, she did the things most mum's do, but at night just before that kiss good night, the stories would come. Family stories… Bible stories…Children's stories…Historical stories…stories about practically everything – or so it seemed to a little boy. The world opened to my eyes through the words spoken by this amazing woman, I was privileged to call 'mother.'

Her family roots were Scottish, but she loved the English. She told me stories of England and London…enough that I had a longing to visit. My father's chosen profession was the ministry – not one that provided much economic freedom. There would not be money to travel and see the world, so my mother's stories would have to suffice. They did, however, light a fire that I carry to this very day!

It happened and more…

I did go to Germany that year, and on the way home spent three days in London! My life was now complete. I felt I could have stayed there forever. Too soon, the time ended and I reluctantly was homeward bound. Not predictable at the time, I have by now found myself in Europe any number of times…a blessing, no doubt!

Several years later, an opportunity came to visit China and Singapore, places I had only heard about, but had occupied a place of curiosity in my heart. My friend Wing Lee arranged for us to visit these exotic places. I remember, a similar feeling I had on my first visit to Europe…until I actually got on the plane and it left the ground, I was unsure whether this was real or a dream!

China was everything I had imagined and so much more…what I imagined had been started by that woman telling stories to a little boy, just before that kiss goodnight…the reality only confirmed the love that had driven those stories.

The dance continues, but changes…

Since that first trip, there have been many more places, all of which have led to the same feelings of anticipation and excitement. In my seventh decade, I still feel the same stirrings in my stomach and heart for the 'unknown' that lies ahead as I buckle my seatbelt preparing for the next adventure.

Something, however, has changed over these years. In the oddest of ways, there has been a shift in the slipstream of time. I am not sure exactly how to express it, but there has been a definite alteration in feelings when traveling.

In the early years (early years being in my forties when I made that first trip), the excitement to go, far outweighed the longing to return home. The 'outbound' simply overwhelmed the 'inbound.' It is not that I didn't look forward to coming home…I did, but it was, well…simply less exciting than heading out.

Somewhere in the mix, a balance developed…meaning; coming home was equally as pleasant a thought as going out. By now, the curve has shifted. I still love to go out – there is little doubt of that – BUT coming home…coming home is as comforting a thought as I can imagine.

To me this is a metaphor for life itself. In the beginning, there is so much going on; there is no time for reflection or thought. Stuff just happens – you will live forever!

As time goes on, and enough things have happened to permit a bit of contemplation, things take on a context. Epictetus says:

"The unexamined life is not worth living, in this way we should never simply accept an impression...but say to it? 'Just a minute; let me see what you are and where you come from.' " – <u>Discourses</u>

As I reflect on my life's journey thus far, thoughts of mortality are unavoidable. A recognition that no matter what has been done or accomplished, there is an end...or is there?

Looking at the unavoidable horizon of life, I find an excitement building for the flight to the next unknown. It is hard to put this into words...indeed, I simply do not have them...BUT as curious as I am about the impending flight from which there is no mortal return...I simply cannot wait to get home!!

THINGS WE FIND AT 40,000 FEET

> "A knower of the Truth
> travels without leaving a trace
> speaks without causing harm
> gives without keeping an account..."
> - Lao Tzu: <u>Tao Te Ching</u>

"Excuse me, is that middle seat taken?"

It started like this...

It was the second leg of a Southwest Airline flight from San Diego to Orlando, Florida – with a stop in Austin, Texas. The day had begun early and the prospects of a one-stop 5-hour flight brought, as it usually does, mixed emotions. No phones, faxes, email – great, but it is a long time to sit.

I don't often fly this airline, because I have lots of miles on a different carrier. Lots of miles means I get on flights early and usually find myself in a pre-assigned exit row with plenty of legroom. When you are 6'4$^{1/2}$" (1.93m) tall, exit rows are golden. On Southwest, you don't get assigned seats, but rather 24 hours prior to your flight – to the minute...no to the second – you check in via the internet.

One imagines thousands of people, just like me, anxiously sitting by their computers with the Airline website open, counting down the seconds. At the strike of the '24-hour window,' you sense the collective and synchronous clicking of the 'check in' button hoping to get a low boarding number. You see, the lower the number, the sooner you get on the aircraft. The sooner you get on the aircraft, the better the seat. There is no assigned seating…it is truly, first come first served.

At the airport, as the flight is called, passengers line up according to their number and file on. You see furtive glances trying to see assignment numbers on the tickets of fellow passengers, making sure someone doesn't jump ahead in the queue. You hear conversations like, "I'm sorry I'm 'A 45,' what is your number?" 'A 46' may have slipped ahead of you, and might say something like, "Oh, the number is close, it doesn't really matter." You might smile and say, "Yeah, you're right, one person doesn't really make a difference." That may be what is said, not what is being thought!!! "What if they get my coveted seat?"

On the plane and in the air…
The flight from San Diego had provided an aisle – not the exit seat, but the first leg was okay. From Austin to Orlando, I captured it…the exit row was mine…I owned it…"Oh Yeah, legroom!"

The other person on the aisle in my row was also a pretty big fellow. The center, however, remained empty long enough that I thought it might stay that way. People don't like center seats; unfortunately when one gets a high category number on this airline, the center seats are pretty much the only option.

An aside…
I can truly sympathize…I once took a flight across on another airline I seldom use. It had assigned seats and I found myself in the back row middle seat. The woman on my left was quite large and the woman on my right even larger – both had mild hygiene issues. You know that thing about how you may not be able to change the circumstance…only your thoughts? This was one of those 'opportunities' for me to exercise that principle…I repeated the phrase uncounted numbers of times on that flight. You know, "…physician heal thyself…!"

Back to the flight…
Austin to Orlando turned out to be unique for an immediate and what turned out to be a delayed reason.

The immediate reason had to do with a fellow in the row behind me on the aisle. He was a little noisy, in fact, quite loud. Suddenly, two airline security people quietly appeared and asked him to come with them – they removed him from the flight.

If one finds themselves being removed from an aircraft, it is a really good thing to not resist and just take your medicine. This fellow understood, and while clearly annoyed he picked up his belongings and got off the plane. He would be allowed to take a later flight. Had he resisted, he would not have flown that day.

With the man behind me gone, what I thought was the last passenger on the flight take his seat. It looked like the center seat on this flight was going to remain open, meaning I would have legroom and good shoulder room…HOT DOG! This comforting thought had just settled in when I heard, "Excuse me, is that middle seat taken?"

I looked up and there was a big fellow about my age looking longingly, and I suppose since it was the last seat on the aircraft, a little desperately at that center seat – it turns out the flight was oversold! When I say a big fellow, I mean he was well north of 6ft (1.8m+) and big boned. He wasn't huge, just a healthy sized man looking to capture that seat. Yep, it wouldn't have been his first choice, maybe so far down his list it wouldn't have been a choice at all, but it was what it was and here we were!

The unexpected…

Bob, as I later learned, settled in and there was little doubt we would dance shoulder to shoulder for the next two or three hours. Airline seats seem to have become a bit narrower over the years. When people with fairly good sized shoulders sit side by side, there are a subtle and ongoing series of adjustments that occur… backward/forward and side to side movements as one tries to be both comfortable and accommodating.

During the climb to altitude, I asked Bob if he were heading out or going home. This is a great way to take the temperature of the person next to you. A lot can be read by the response to that question.

Then it happened...
Bob was going out...he was going out to a meeting of 'Fun Park' exhibitors at the Orlando Convention Center. Fun parks...fun park exhibitors??? What??

There was little doubt he had 'set the hook.'

I have met lots of people on airplanes in the two million plus miles I have flown over the years...milk salesmen, button collectors, artists, musicians, tons of computer sales/service people, leather experts, moms/dads, students and athletes, but this was my first Fun Park owner...shoot, I had never even heard of Fun Parks. Sure I knew of big amusement parks, traveling carnivals, and maybe a smaller water park or two, but a Fun Park AND companies that supported this business was a revelation...both entertaining and informative.

He had begun with a small service station, built a restaurant, put in another service station, along with a couple of franchise businesses (Subway and maybe MacDonald's – those parts of the conversation a little hazy)...but it was the piece of land he owned in rural Texas, where he put in a Fun Park, that I found almost curious.

He spoke about his business and how in an economy that was hurting, a Fun Park provided a few hours of recreation, at a price point that met the need.

What made it better was the quiet and thoughtful way he talked about it. He was one of those small business entrepreneurs who don't get noticed in all of the rhetoric of Washington and Wall Street...one of those small business entrepreneurs upon whose shoulders this country has been built...one of those small business entrepreneurs who loves his country, his business and the people he serves. The kind of fellow you would like to see talked about on the news as an example for other citizens, rather than those who have caused us such enormous problems through greed and selfishness.

While learning about his business, I pulled out my computer and shared a little of what I was going to be presenting the following day. Even though it was a clinical level presentation, Bob got it and said, "You might not think I learned anything from our conversation, but I sure did." "Me too – from you." I thought.

Is this going anywhere?

You know, life brings things in the most unexpected ways. Here were a couple of fellows, about the same age who just 'found a place' with each other. It wasn't about Fun Parks or my work really, although those topics provided the vehicle for our interaction. It was one of those moments in life where two older guys, who had a fairly common 'time on planet' and 'cultural exposure,' found a comfortable and engaging resonance. The conversation didn't need much extra explanation to set contexts, it was just like putting on an old pair of tennis shoes…you know, comfortable on the feet.

Life gets busy…there are lots of things still, gratefully, to do. It is just a really nice thing when you find one of those friction free mature interactions with another human being…where after you have spent some of your spirit, you feel refreshed.

Sometimes it's the middle seats in life, the places where the legroom is not so comfy, when you find yourself shoulder to shoulder with a stranger, that provide the reward unexpected. I had the legroom, he had the middle seat and we were a bit shoehorned in shoulder to shoulder, but I'll bet if you asked Bob…a comfortable flight was had by all.

TWO STORIES MAKE ONE

> "So long as the memory of certain beloved friends
> lives in my heart, I shall say that life is good."
> - Helen Keller

It was usually at the end of the day. Dinner over…homework done…the small routines complete…bed and a good night's sleep on everyone's mind.

On those special nights, the sounds began to gently fill the house. It started with some sort of chord progression…poking around…looking for the right key – then it would start.

He couldn't read a note of music, but he had a gift. He could reach somewhere deep inside…the place where few ever see the landscape of the soul. Hunting, pecking the notes, looking for the 'sweet spot,' and then…and then, something magical would come.

Longing…tender…thoughtful…familiar – words fail, for who can describe the beauty that comes from the richly developed hand of the artist when he or she simply gets out of the way and lets another spirit take control.

Ministry – a guarded profession…

My father was a passionate man. In his chosen profession it needed to be a controlled passion. Sunday mornings, from the pulpit there was little doubt the things he said were more than just words.

The struggle of preparation…attention to detail…the uncertainty one feels week after week when they take center stage for those needing to be fed. The torrents of his spirit would come spilling out like a small break in a dam desperately trying, yet failing, to contain the water pressure behind it.

There were few who heard him preach who would not remember those soaring moments of freedom, so much more feeding for him than the congregants in those Sunday morning pews. The people would melt from before his eyes as he was transformed and transported to a different place known only to him and his God. This, in fact, is what he lived for.

Passionate people, if they find themselves in public professions, often need to be a bit careful. They wear their feelings and emotions close to the surface. While all of us admire them, they sometimes can be overwhelming. For my father, the ministry had been the vehicle to 'break' the wild bucking horse that had lacked focus and direction. My mother, of course, was the other force in his life. Out his love for her and for Christ – neither of whom could he survive without – he had learned to channel his energy and talents.

While to many he seemed to be a tower of strength, he was really no different than they. His congregations would have been surprised to see him grunting and stamping his feet while watching the televised Friday night fights…his vicarious blood lust satisfied by two men beating one another mercilessly. He seemed to know how to find outlets for the complex and churning waters of his soul.

But then there was the music…the music. During his earlier years, he had been on the radio playing a number of instruments and singing. It was the piano, however, that was his seductress. It was the piano that would bring him back again and again. Somewhat of a showman – I suppose one cannot be a minister without that trait – he enjoyed playing for small church meetings and other gatherings.

There was his time…
The late evenings, however, were something entirely different. Here he was not playing for others. He played for his God…he

106

played for his Christ…he played for the life of his very soul. Public playing for him was a monologue. Not so here…his touch to the keyboard was a conversation, a duet with the unseen hand of his Creator.

Sometimes as I lay in bed reading waiting to be taken by the gods of sleep, the siren sounds of my father's hand would come reaching deeply into parts of me…freeing parts of me…holding court in parts of me. Sometimes I would get up and quietly slip behind the door of the piano room just to listen – for this dance was personal, intimate…not to be disturbed. The sounds, the rhythms, the freedom of shifting keys seemingly with no resolution in sight…only to hear the reflections of what he felt find an unpredicted chord resolution and a soft landing that could have been accomplished by no other hand. When he finished playing, he would sit for sometime in quiet thought and gratitude for having danced with his Maker.

I had not thought of my father's playing for many years.

The turning page…

I have a relatively new friend in Brenham, Texas. We 'accidently' found ourselves sitting on a flight from Houston, Texas to Orlando a little over a year ago. It was one of those chance meetings that led to a little more…then a little more. We found ourselves in Dallas earlier this year and spent a little more time. We had been looking for an opportunity to visit again, and as fate would have it a circumstance arrived. I was in Austin, Texas for a conference just a few miles from his home. After a long week on the road, and after the meeting, Molly and I headed a few miles east to Brenham. I was looking forward to seeing Bob, but I was tired.

We arrived in the morning, and as that wonderful Texas hospitality dictates, we were welcomed as members of the family. After putting our bags away, we settled in for a chat and a great cup of coffee. As we were about to leave for a sightseeing drive around Brenham, Molly slipped out for a few minutes. I had seen the piano when we entered the living room, and asked who played. He said he did and wondered if I would like to hear something. "Yes, I would be delighted."

Bob reads music and said, "I kind of like this arrangement, and thought I would share it with you."

With that, his practiced hand began to play "The Old Rugged Cross." The arrangement was not straightforward…the ebb and flow of the music not predictably clear, but when the piece resolved, it came to a soft landing only the arranger could have seen in his mind.

Bob, of course, could not have known the untold number of times I had heard my father play that piece…in those quiet and intimate moments when he thought he was alone in the music room of our home.

That moment, in the home of my new friend Bob, as his gentle fingers played a unique arrangement of an old gospel piece, I closed my eyes and was transported into the presence of my father…to the presence of our common Father and the spirit he found so deeply in his soul – and mine.

It's nice to be reminded…

For those who do not appreciate the existence of a creative, living, moving and engaging intelligent spirit of the universe, I feel a bit of sadness. This gentle soul in Brenham, Texas knew nothing of my life or background, but simply felt to share a bit of himself with a newly found friend. He could have had no idea the depth of my spirit this arrangement, of an old Gospel Hymn, touched. He could have had no idea I had been transported to a time forty years earlier as my father's gift gifted hand and our Father's spirit lifted us both. He could have had no idea.

Life counts…

The Biblical scripture, dare I say, all spiritual writings teach us that in our weakness we find stability and strength. They teach us that we only truly can know when we let go. They teach us that in the quietness of listening we find the majesty of the universal sound and resonance in the spiritual fabric of our collective humanity.

The Old Rugged Cross?? Meaningful to my life?? Of this Bob knew nothing...nor did he need to. He listened to 'his heart' and reached deeply into mine...

RANDOM ACTS

"If you love somebody, you had
better hurry up and tell them."
– Author Unknown

He was riding his bicycle on the service road just off Interstate 5 when a car left the freeway, came down an embankment and hit him straight on!

What are the odds??

I'm not sure what the fellow was thinking when he got up that morning and headed out for a ride. I am not sure what the woman driver was thinking as she headed north on the interstate. I am certain, neither one of them expected to find themselves in proximity under any circumstances!

Maybe the guy was thinking about work, or breakfast, or his family or the music he was listening to…the woman hurrying to work or the store or coming home from dropping off her kids…whatever. Of all the things these two people could have conceived, in their wildest imaginations…the darkest places in the depths of their brains…this…this would NEVER have emerged into their consciousness, and yet here it was…their lives would never be the same, and I mourned for them.

Why them? Why then? Why not someone else? Why not somewhere else? Why not one minute sooner or one minute later? The unpredictability and random acts of life exceed storylines that even the most creative writers could dig out of the recesses of their minds.

This could have been anyone…it could have not happened at all.

A memory…
It was Vietnam…the early fall of 1969 and by now nearly a year of my tour had passed. I had found ways to compensate for being in this strange land. A prime example was learning to sleep. I had self-talked that I was safe, that if something happened it would be to someone else. Fantasy? Sure, but one does whatever it takes to normalize in the most abnormal of situations.

I was an air traffic controller in the military and had adapted to the unnatural sounds of airplanes landing on a runway not more than 200 yards (183m) from my 'hooch' – the name for the plywood barracks in which we were housed.

Sleeping was also challenged during the rainy season. There is little louder than the mind numbing decibels of monsoon rains hitting a metal roof. One had to practically yell to hold a conversation with the person next to them. Even then I found a way to touch that gracious 'gift of the gods' and fall asleep.

It is said there are two categories of people in this world…those that move dirt, and those that supervise the dirt movers. In Vietnam, we moved a lot of dirt.

It had been a late night, and I had spent the evening at the non-commissioned officer's (NCO) club with my best friend Bob – I slept hard.

They said the hooch took a direct hit…the navy commander probably hadn't heard a thing and had been killed outright. They said it was his last day 'in country.' He was preparing to head home…no mission to fly, but a flight to catch departing this airfield for the last, "Thank God Almighty" time.

I wondered about that man and wrote some of these thoughts then...

What had he been thinking as he counted down the days. I wondered how many missions he had flown and how many times his life had been at risk...I wondered how often he had thanked God for a safe return to base and the cold beer in his hand to celebrate another day burned from the calendar.

There were rituals...

We did this you know...we counted days...we celebrated when there were fewer left than there had been to stay – at first the fear of too many days ahead, with too many chances...chances for something bad to happen; then too few days with heightened sense of excitement that home grew closer, but fear that it would be snatched away at the last minute. Even getting on that plane with 200 plus other dirty smelly GIs at the end of the tour, ran the risk of being shot down as the aircraft took off. No sir, no sigh of relief until the airspace of the Republic of South Vietnam was somewhere in the distance behind us.

Continuing the thought...

In the early morning hours, the navy commander's life was snatched away at the last minute...he would not be catching that flight home...at least not the one he had been anticipating. The string of life severed from 'his instrument' in the universe, no longer resonating in measured harmony with anything...with anyone.

I wondered what he might have been thinking as he got up that morning. Maybe he had been dreaming of his family and how great it would be to breathe the fresh and familiar air of his hometown. Maybe he was sitting on the edge of his bed putting on his boots, in uniform for the last time...looking forward.

I didn't hear the rockets. I had learned to sleep...sleep in this 'Alice Through the Looking Glass' country, through most anything. Me? I was dreaming about my family at home and how great it would be to breathe the fresh and familiar air of my hometown. On that morning I sat on the edge of the bed, put on my jungle boots, in uniform for yet another day and headed for breakfast.

When I heard the news, I was struck by the complete and utter unpredictability of life…He was gone, his family's lives would never be the same, and I mourned him.

The car did not come off the freeway that year and hit my bicycle…it hit that navy commander's. I wondered, why his hooch, not mine? Why him, not me? Why not later or sooner?

Each of us has stories of the randomness of life…the unexpected moments that change everything. Not all are lethal…many act to change life in the most remarkable of ways…These kinds of things, however, remind me to appreciate and try and be as much in the 'moment' as possible…because one never knows…

THE STRING NO LONGER VIBRATES

"…For what is your life? It is even a vapour,
that appeareth for a little time,
and then vanisheth away."
- James 4:14: <u>Bible</u>

"…and in the end, it's not the
years in your life that count.
It's the life in your years.
- Abraham Lincoln

"Please forward this as I don't have access to all reunion addresses on my phone."

And so it was that I learned of the death of one of my high school classmates. The subject line of the email read: "Arrangements for Dick Johnston."

A different time and place…
It was 1957 and our family had just moved to Fairmont, West Virginia from Cleveland, Ohio…more precisely from Euclid, Ohio where my father pastored the Euclid Avenue Baptist Church. It was a small congregation of 300 or so souls, and his first pastorate in the United States.

We had come from Toronto in 1951 in the night. If our first 'Green Card' pictures were any indication, we looked to be Eastern European immigrants rather than a small family unit a mere 285 miles from the city in which we were born and my parents had grown up. There was excitement, however, in this new land with similar language and only nuanced differences from the country of the Union Jack – the flag subsequently replaced by the Maple Leaf.

We spent six years in Euclid in a lower middle class neighbourhood, where the parishioners were factory workers, bus drivers, mailmen and other such folk. Good people…hard working people.

A little religious background…

The Baptist Church – that would be 'American Baptists' – does not have much of an organizational infrastructure. The '…First Great [spiritual] Awakening…' had swept the American Colonies in the early 1700s. While Baptists had been around since the late 1700s, it was a split, with what became the Southern Baptists, during the 'Second Great Awakening' in the mid-1800's, that the American Baptists found their own feet.

Baptist churches are independent, meaning they are each responsible for their own affairs including the recruitment of new ministers. When they have a need, they send a small group of elders to hear someone preach somewhere. The visit is not necessarily announced. When they find a minister they like, they invite him to preach in their church…you know, to 'squeeze the melon' to see if it is ripe and a good fit. If it all works, an offer is made, negotiated and a deal done.

So it was that Dad was visited by the First Baptist Church of Fairmont, West Virginia in 1957 and before we knew it, we headed into those "…almost heaven…" West Virginia Hills, and our assigned home at 912 8th Street where we would reside through my high school years.

A place to find a friend…

Once settled, it was off to a new school…new people, and peculiar new southern accents to understand. Butcher Elementary was the starting place. There were two things that stood out about that school:

- The fire escape was a circular slide from the upper floors to the ground, and

- Dick Johnston was my first friend

It wasn't that I made any effort to befriend him…I was new and pretty uncomfortable. He simply captured me and treated me as though he and I had known each other our whole lives. Even at that age, he seemed to have that way about him…a comfort with practically everyone. Dick had made me his friend, and that gave me credibility with the other kids.

He lived on 1st street near the bridge on Fairmont Avenue and I lived on 8th street near the high school. There is little doubt his presence made my transition to this new community as seamless as it possibly could have been. In the second year, just before junior high, he and another youngster, came with my family to our cottage in Canada for a week or so. You see Dick wasn't just my first friend in Fairmont, but the only friend I had had to that point in my life.

The river flows…

As junior high turned into high school, athletics took over most of my discretionary time, and while Dick and I remained friends, the time we spent together became less and less frequent. After high school we lost touch, and it wasn't until my 40th class reunion that we saw one another again.

When we met that year and caught up with one another's lives, I learned he had suffered some significant health challenges, but that smile, the twinkle in his eye, the genuineness of his spirit transported me almost immediately to the playground at Butcher school when it seemed that he had always been in my life.

I experienced a twinge of regret that I had not gotten to know him in his adult life…the wine had matured…clearly richer, wiser and even more thoughtful – I had missed something.

Subject: Arrangements for Dick…

The funeral home had a website with an electronic guestbook you could sign…I left a note, and as I read the comments from so many others, it was clear Dick had touched a lot of lives with the same spirit I had felt, lo those many years ago. It wasn't that I was special…it was his spirit that made me feel special…a gift…a gift he undoubtedly cultivated his entire life.

There is something about early connections in life…something about the sparkle of youth…something about the genuine and authentic spirit that never diminishes. This week I found myself transported to another place…another time…and wept for that fearless little boy who had made me his friend…

SOMEBODY TOUCHED ME

> "Touch has a memory."
> – John Keats

He was a small man in a well-worn brown suit, sitting alone in circular waiting room. He had been glancing at the book in his hand, then gazing to some distant place…returning to the book again.

The Big Easy…

I had been in New Orleans for a three-day training program at one of the local downtown hospitals. Rather than staying in the city, the hotel was in Metairie twenty minutes or so away. While things are coming back – other than the downtown tourist areas – most everywhere else in the city is still undergoing substantial rehabilitation.

Folks often think traveling to these kinds of places is exciting and in some cases sort of exotic. For the less traveled, let me explain. It goes like this: Up and at it for breakfast around 6:30AM. Work through the day…finish up after dark…eat dinner somewhere in the late 7PM to early 8PM hours, finishing an hour or so later. That leaves a little time to read and tuck in to start the cycle once again. It is incredibly exotic!!

The event…

We were waiting for security to open a small conference room, where the morning would be spent team teaching a course on the management of chronic back and neck pain. In the 10 minutes or so during 'the wait,' I watched this fellow repeat the cycle of eye to book…eye to some distant place…eye back to the book. He read a few words and appeared to think a little about what he had read.

The guard came and as we started toward the room, I walked by the fellow and noted he was in the scriptures – he was '…redeeming his time…' while waiting for a doctor's appointment.

As I passed he looked up and our eyes briefly met. "What book are you reading?" I asked. He looked a bit startled, refocusing his eyes, "Luke Chapter 8." He replied. "What's it saying?" I followed.

In a halting rhythmic rich Haitian/English – the French accent oozing compellingly from his tongue – he began to recite the story of the woman who had had an issue of blood for 12 years, and could find no relief. She believed if she touched Christ's garment she would be healed…so she did and the scripture says she was healed.

Just then, the man was called for his appointment and he stood. I said to him, "Do you know what the next few scriptures say?" He shook his head no. "Not yet."

I replied, "Christ says, 'Somebody touched me.'" To which his disciples replied, that he was in a crowd with many people touching him. Christ responded, "Somebody touched ME," for he had felt virtue come out of him.

It was not a handshake…it was not a pat on the back…it was an intimate connection to his spiritual body…a transfer of spirit understood by every parent who calms an upset child through the touch of their hand, a look of safety as their eyes connect, or the warmth of the bond when holding one another.

In that instant and interchange, the universe stopped for the two of us. We looked into each other's eyes for the briefest of moments…excellent moments…a common and transcendent bridge of communication. In that ever so fleeting connection…there was no time.

We shook hands smiled, nodded in acknowledgement and off we

went to our respective days.

It was good...

My life seems to be filled with little moments like this. I suppose, in some ways, I look for them. I sometimes think maybe it is because God knows how frail I am and that I need them...need them to be reinforced that there 'is' meaning...to appreciate the interconnectedness of the human spirit...to be reminded in spite of being bombarded with negativity, separation and self-interest, we are all part of the same tapestry of humanity.

There is so much I don't know...so much I do not understand...so much that escapes my sense of life. Stepping away, in an attempt to gather significance from the big picture often overwhelms me.

But then...then I see a small man sitting on the edge of a circular waiting room, glancing at the book in his hand, gazing to some distant place. We exchange a few words from a text we have in common, and we find a 'place.'

It doesn't matter we will never see one another again...it doesn't matter we know nothing about each other's lives...nothing matters really except this...

He touched 'Me!'

IT ONLY TAKES A MOMENT

"When people take some step to enlarge a fellow citizen's property,
or advance his career, there are several different
motives...It could be sheer goodwill...respect....
or he may inspire their confidence..."
- Cicero M The Good Life: On Duties

"Would you like that cappuccino to be a double sir?"

I had been walking around the exhibit area looking for a booth that was serving coffee, and there she was looking for a customer – need and fulfillment...I like that.

The professional society to which I have belonged for the past 23 years or so is made up of pretty high-end performers. Most of them are spine surgeons, preoccupied with their practices and the economics that go along with this kind of work. The exhibit areas for these meetings are huge, and while not all...mostly consist of vendors displaying surgical instruments and hardware for spinal surgery.

The meet...
This particular company's display had an espresso stand and a smiling young woman doing the job for which she had been hired – making specialty coffees.

I was the only person in line at the moment, so while I waited, I asked her if she were a student. "No," she said, "I have a degree in music, but have moved home to Chicago to be closer to the family. It is hard to find work in my field, so I pick up what I can." Now I was curious.

I told her my older sister taught voice in Washington, D.C....an opera singer...a soprano...and singing as well, maybe better than ever in her life. Anne has a solid reputation and a stable of 50 or so students and a waiting list. I have teased her over the years about being a 'semi-professional' singer, to which she has chided, "I am a professional singer and teacher!" In fact she is, and in spite of the fact that I don't often tell her – or at least tell her enough, I am extremely proud of her chosen profession and her gift...for truly she is gifted.

A gift – a present...

Ah yes, the gift...that brings us back to this young girl at the cappuccino machine. I asked her range; she said soprano....just like my sister...but her interest was in Baroque music. While I have little knowledge about different music styles, I'm pretty sure Baroque carries strong rhythms, consistent moods, with more than one line of melody...I hope for my sake, and my sister's critique this description passes muster!

As this young woman talked about her love of music, the moderately polite and flat look in her eye lit up like a well-decorated tree on Christmas morning. She shared what singing meant to her and how she missed performing.

When I asked why she wasn't singing, she said "Since moving back to Chicago, I have been away from the my music community, and it just isn't the same."

I couldn't resist "Are you any good?" I asked. Without hesitation she replied, "Yes I am, I am very good."

Her answer wasn't that kind of uninformed bragging that often comes with youth or ignorance. It was simply what it was, and came with a touch of spirit that had respect for the gift and confidence painted all over it...

["I love this craft!" she continued. "It feeds me. I miss not being as engaged as I have been in the past. I don't care about recognition...I just want to sing!"]

She actually didn't say any of that, she just said, "Yes I am. I am very good." The rest is the commentary of what I felt when she spoke the words. Singing was good for her...did anything else matter – really?

I told her I had taught university for a number of years, and always encouraged my students that they could do whatever they wanted in life. Maybe in the field for which they were preparing – maybe not – BUT if they followed their hearts, they would find their 'place.' If they had a gift and faith, they could do anything.

"Chasing your heart is risky," I said. "When you do this, there is little to hide behind...little place to take cover...convention makes little difference in matters of the heart you know...yeah, you know."

A point – for me...

Then came THE MOMENT. The kind that provides perspective...the moment when you connect with another human being at an elemental level...where age, training, experience, attitudes, professions, mean nothing. The unknown, unrehearsed and unexpected instant when two human beings find a mutual connection in time, and little else matters.

I asked her if she were gifted...she knew she was...so I said, "...why aren't you honoring the gift?" She repeated her parents wanted her to be close and she felt an obligation to the family.

I asked her again...A tear formed in the corner of her right eye, and a lump in my chest.

She said, "Because I am afraid." In that brief moment, we were connected and I mean connected. "I'm afraid it might not be what I think."

She wouldn't know, of course, if she didn't try, and the only way to know would be to act.

She said, "Wow, I wasn't expecting this!" "Nor was I," said I. "But here we are." We held eyes silently for a few seconds, and knew whatever had transpired had meaning...for both of us.

The moment passed...

I thanked her for the cappuccino – the double shot – and turned to leave. I looked back and gently said, "Honor the gift," and with a smile began to move away. "I will" she said, "I will...I needed that, and thank you."

"You don't know," I thought.. "For it is I who should be thanking you."

I smiled again and headed off, hot drink in hand and a song...a song in my heart...the rhythm strong; the mood elevated and consistent...the melody, well, in this case harmony, and it was close and tight.

What really matters?

It's hard to know when one is going to be rewarded in life...when those small, seemingly commonplace events become something more... something much more.

I will never see this young woman again, and don't know whether the touch we both experienced will have any lasting meaning for her. I can only speak for me. It often isn't life's boulders we work to move that make the difference in our daily existence...sometimes it's just taking the time to turn over the pebbles.

I wouldn't know this girl again if I sat or stood next to her – nor she me – but maybe one day I will hear her sing. Maybe something in that gift will reach into my heart a second time and I will recognize that harmony again.

CHILDREN PLAY

"Suffer the little children to come unto me…
for of such is the kingdom of God"
- Mark 10:14 Bible

I had been lost in thought as I sat in the gardens when I heard a little girl cry out, "Je vois, je vois, je vois une voiture verte" [I see, I see, I see a green car] This was quickly followed by the voice of a gentleman saying, "Non, non, je ne vois pas une voiture verte !" [No, no I don't see a green car!]

The little girl, and another said, "Oui, oui, oui." [Yes, yes, yes] To which the man replied, "non, non, non." [No, no, no] This back and forth continued a couple more times with both the little girls and the older gentleman laughing and giggling together.

Finally he said, "Ah, maintenant je vois la voiture verte !," [Ah, now I see the green car] and the little girls squealed with delight. One of them then said, "Maintenant tu grand-papa,"[Now you grandfather], as it was his turn to find something. I forgot what I had been thinking about and was mesmerized by this man and his grandchildren.

It was Paris and the Luxembourg Gardens where I had come to a rest after walking around the city for most of the morning. Entering the grounds on a long tree lined walkway toward the Luxembourg Palace and reflecting pool I had found myself a resting bench when I heard the children's voices. My French is "…pas trés bien…" [not very good], but I understood this. I found myself quietly playing right along and looking for the things the children and the grandfather pointed out.

Yesterday, all my troubles seemed so far away..

I was taken instantly to my childhood where my mother had taught me a similar game called, "I spy with my little eye, something that is _____ (fill in a color). My mother would pick moderately challenging things for me to find, and I would choose ones I thought she would never get…we both did well – me because of her skill in making me work, but not too hard, and she for her naturally quick eye from which I could keep nothing hidden! The language was different, the country and continent far, far away…but the lessons? The life lessons were not.

Gardens – different, but the same…

Molly and I were on our morning walk around the neighborhood of Allied Gardens where we live in San Diego. Our standard, nearly four-mile route, takes us through our community park – not quite the halfway point. On Saturday mornings, it is full of people in varying sized groups.

What triggered the memory of Luxembourg Gardens was the number of children playing with their parents or grandparents. There were small groups playing soccer to the sounds of, "Great kick!" or "Wait, wait, kick it this way!" Teaching…if not completely 'teachable moments.'

There was a mother reading to her child under a tree, and a small girl reading to her mother on a park bench from one of those electronic books. A dad tossing a football to his little son…a mum swinging her daughter back and forth on the swings…a group of children free-style playing at once on the slide, now the swings and monkey bars – unaware they were under the watchful eye of their parents. Everywhere we looked the guardians playing with/instructing their children. The struggle, the passion, the joy, the success, the failure…all of it…all of it right there for the seeing.

Life's playground

What struck me the most was the commonality and community of man. In many ways, this wasn't Paris or Allied Gardens, but the metaphor for life – early or late '…in the ground of play.'

Isn't that the way it is? Don't we move back and forth in the roles of child and parent…teacher and student. Isn't this part of the secret for all of us? At first being given artificial goals – priming the pump, as it were – until we find that 'thing' into which we can pour our interests and desires? The ignited passion driving us even further – as the teachers and mentors we have had become part of the inner school, motivating us to ask more questions…to play the game at a higher and more subtle level.

The surprise…

There was a time when I thought, as I grew older I would look wistfully at scenes like this and remember similar events in my life – but no more. The mystery, or secret is that it never changes, if one chooses to continue to show up "…Saturday morning in the park…" There will always be mentors and teachers looking for students to mold and shape and help to grow. Once one question is answered, there will be many more to occupy one's attention.

When does a person stop learning? When does one stop playing the game? Where is the point where one says, "Well, now I understand…now I get it!" If one is to remain alive, the answer, of course is…NEVER.

While I am not ancient, as the span of life is concerned, I am surely slipping down the slope toward its end – at least as time in service on this planet is concerned. What is it that I want more than anything else for the time that is remaining? The eternal and needful driving interest to find that "…voiture verte…"

THE PHANTOM FIVE

"Men do not quit playing because they grow old;
they grow old because they quit playing"
– Oliver Wendell Holmes

It might have been 2006...maybe 2007...I am uncertain.

What I am certain about is that they were children then, by now
they would be a young adults. Nina (as in singer Nina Simone) and
Ella (as in Fitzgerald – also a very famous singer)...in fact, I couldn't
wait to see them.

It began like this...
In 1996, I was given my first opportunity to speak overseas. It is
one of those events in life about which you remember almost
everything. It had begun in the back of a ballroom of the La Jolla
Marriot Hotel, in the fall of 1994. The lighting in the room was
muted, a small circle of chairs gathered, and some quiet conversation
about a conference that would take place in Würzburg, Germany in
March of 1996. The fellow leading the conversation was setting up
the meeting and he invited me to speak. With little hesitation, I
accepted.

With the exception of Vietnam in the late 1960s, this would be my
first adventure overseas. In contrast to that experience, nobody in
Germany had an interest in ending my life prematurely!

As the flight came in for a landing in Frankfurt, it struck me this
was really happening. From there it would be a train to Würzburg

and the Congress – I was excited!

It was there I met Chris, an energetic physical therapist (physiotherapist) working for the company sponsoring the meeting. It became clear this young woman was key to the conference success. She was everywhere...checking everything... eyes on all of it. All went well, and I thought I had reached the peak of my professional career. I wanted to savor every moment of everything. Little did I know this was just the beginning...

Many years and conferences passed...
A decade or so later, I was in Zürich to visit my friend Werner on business. While there, Chris and her hubby David invited me to dinner in their home. By now they were parents of two delightful young girls – Nina and Ella – both with sparkling eyes that reflected a keen intelligence taken from their parents.

I genuinely love children. There are so many things about them that seize the imagination. Often, it is difficult to make a connection when time is brief, so I have developed a couple of techniques that work well. I crouch down so that I am at eye level with them. This is helpful because I am a tall fellow and it is easy to intimidate youngsters by size alone. The second, and most successful over the years is "The Phantom five!" I am uncertain how it ended up in my toolkit. Perhaps it came out of my own mind or from someone skilled in working with youngsters. All I know is that it is the best thing I have ever discovered when connecting with children.

It works like this...
"Give me five," says one person to the other, and they slap open palms together. Young kids like to do this, old folks sometimes too...

My variation is called the "Phantom five." Sometimes it takes a little non-threatening encouragement...almost always

starting by crouching down.

I hold out one finger and say, "Just for **fun**, give me **one**." The youngster puts out one finger and I slap it gently with my single finger. In return, they slap mine.

Then I hold out two fingers and say, "Just for **you**, give me **two**." A two finger slap follows.

The progression continues… "Just for **me**, give me **three**." "Just once **more**, give me **four**." "Man **alive**, give me **five**."

One would think that's the end, because by now the child is engaged and both parties are having fun. Ah, not so…the best part is yet to come. The BEST part is the "Phantom five."

This is a little harder to explain in words, but you say, "Now give me the Phantom five!" and raise your hand as though you were going to give a 'high five.' BUT…and this IS the best part…you miss the child's hand in a dramatic fashion! Get it?? You miss hands…the slap doesn't actually happen…you swish the air! It is the PHANTOM FIVE!

At first, the youngster generally looks a little confused, but then you repeat just the Phantom five and say something like, "Isn't that great!!" For some unknown reason, they catch on and almost always smile broadly…maybe if you're lucky they laugh a little.

By now they usually want to do it a couple more times from "Just for fun, give me one" through the "Now give me the Phantom five." The energy you give to the slap that whooshes through the air is what they can't wait to get to! Almost without fail it creates a connection and a new friend has been made.

It still works…

Three weeks ago I was in Zürich again. Knowing I would be there, I emailed David and Chris to see if we might have dinner. I wouldn't be alone. A dear family friend from Detroit, living in Stuttgart, Germany drove down to spend a day exploring the city. They invited both of us over for dinner.

Nina no longer lives at home, and Ella had a busy schedule the day we planned to come, but they both made it – Nina in her early twenties and Ella in her late teens. Nina came first and I kind of awkwardly did just the last part of the air swishing "Phantom five." When Ella arrived from a strenuous bike ride home, I was better and we did the whole deal…both had remembered it.

Dinner was simply wonderful and the hospitality could not have been better. We had rich and lively conversation, and to the credit of these amazing young women, they stayed up, completely engaged in the discussions, until 12:30AM. As we were leaving Ella and I did the Phantom five once more. "Do it again," she said as if she wanted to get it clearly in her mind. We did, both smiled, laughed and I felt the connection we had discovered several years before. The neural pathways laid down remained and there was a reward for both of us. I suspect we will find a spot for this little ritual when we see one another again. I am in hopes it will become a part of her toolkit too.

It's about the moment isn't it?

I am uncertain when I will see my Swiss friends again…one never knows. I know this, however, the connection with the girls was (is) still alive. There is something else about that "Phantom five" I usually don't confess. The kids think it is for them, because it makes them smile and laugh, and it surely provides for a quick pathway for openness and trust.

In truth, however, I do it for me. There is little in life that gives me more pleasure than connecting with a young mind devoid of so many of the burdens life brings with it. Moments with children remind me of the child I have inside of me and the importance of keeping it alive, open and engaged. They remind me, not of the paradise lost of adulthood and maturity, but of the hope and energy of a life yet to be lived – mine!

"Hey, just for fun give me one…"

IT'S HARDLY EVER WHAT YOU THINK

> "A sudden bold and unexpected question doth many
> times surprise a man and lay him open."
> - Francis Bacon

It was 2:30PM Central time and the taxi was heading to O'Hare international airport in Chicago. The conversation was collegial until he mentioned a couple of influences in his life...his father and the small town in which he had grown up...

This is about the serendipity of life...the unpredictable...the emergent gift from the landscape of experience...so unexpected as to overwhelm one in the moment – so intricately woven, in the broader manuscript, as to cause one to fall on their knees and cry to the Creator of the universe, "I am unworthy."

Gotta back this up a little...
It had begun with the loss of my friend, colleague and mentor Vert, an orthopedic surgeon who had influenced his field for decades. His sudden departure at the hands of a single vehicle car crash stunned all of us – family...friends...colleagues.

Over the years, I had become a surrogate member of the family and was asked to perform the eulogy at his memorial service...and so on a November day in 2009 a group of friends and colleagues from all over the world came to bid farewell to <u>their</u> friend. The house was full...as were our hearts.

A week or so after the memorial, I got a call from a fellow at the

North American Spine Society (NASS) who had attended the service, asking whether I might give a small presentation regarding Vert at the annual convention.

After speaking I met a physician named Jeff, an Asian American academic orthopedist from UCLA. We had a few polite words about Vert, and moved on. There was something about this fellow that caught my attention, but the meeting was busy and the orbits of our daily lives quite different.

A little more of Vert...

Vert had, for many years, co-organized a scientific meeting on low back and pelvic pain. His colleague was a fellow, richly respected and a well-published academic from the Netherlands. This meeting occurs every three years at some international location – in 2010 it was Los Angeles. I was asked to give a brief memorial lecture to the Congress.

It turned out Jeff was also speaking there, and we had a few moments to chat once again...this time without the demands of work and of our busy schedules. As before, I felt a draw to this man...there was something about his spirit I resonated with.

Then there was Dallas...

This year I was asked to co-chair the 2012 North American Spine Society meeting in Dallas in October. Part of the responsibilities for this job involved a site visit in February. Jeff, also one of the co-chairs for the meeting, came to Dallas, where we found ourselves visiting sites and getting to know one another a little better in a relaxed setting. It was interesting to watch him work with the others on the team.

Subsequent to this I participated in a couple of planning conference calls he led, and noted again the deliberate clarity and inclusiveness with which he worked.

Then there was Chicago...

Earlier this week, there was a meeting in Chicago to finalize the program. This is a complicated scientific meeting with lots of sessions, symposia, special interest groups, podium presentations and posters.

We started at 8:30AM and to my surprise by 2PM we were finished. I had expected to be taking work home, but in fact under Jeff's consensus driven leadership, a surprisingly complicated juggling act was completed – and in less than the allotted time.

My flight home was at 8:35PM, but I realized that I might be able to get to O'Hare and stand-by on an earlier flight. I heard Jeff say he was heading that way and suggested we share the cab. The drive would be about 35 minutes and I was looking forward to getting to know him a little better; maybe even a sense of the resonance I felt with him.

Okay, we're getting to the good stuff…
Because he is Asian American, I wondered if his demeanour had come from cultural influences. I've traveled a few times in China and the East and find the culture there compelling. After commenting on my perception of his leadership style, I asked him what he thought had influenced him. He said, of course, his father who had been a university professor, and the community in which he had grown up.

It is surprising where one's mind goes. In the flash of a millisecond, I envisioned him nurtured in an Asian community where everyone – friends and relatives – brought a sense of the universe to him.

What he said, however, was: "It was a small town you have probably never heard of – Fairmont, West Virginia."

The punch line…
For those reading this who won't grasp the impact of these words…I spent the most formative 14 years or so of my life in the rich culture of a small, coal mining supported, West Virginia town…in Marion county…nestled along the banks of the Monongahela (Mon-on-ga-hê-la) river – Fairmont!

I was practically speechless and said, "You have got to be kidding me. I grew up there too!!" The moment of revelation stunned both of us!

Who could conceive we shared a common town, high school, athletic experience and some common friends – me the class of '65...he the class of '83.

Let me put this in perspective, if indeed there is any possible way to do so. There were a series of totally unrelated events that led to the two of us sitting in that taxi on the way to the airport. There are legion of reasons why the conversation should never have happened...yet here we were!

My parents planted a '...curiosity of the casual moment...' that has provided me with the most remarkable life experiences – this no exception! Without the curiosity, the questions would never have been asked...we would have ridden to the airport and headed home – "...ships passing in the night..." BUT that is NOT what happened!

I can't speak for those who do not believe in the active engagement of God in the Universe. I surely understand bringing spiritual matters into question – God knows I have spent plenty of my life asking and wondering about them...

Yet, the moment of revelation, in the back seat of that taxi this week – so absolutely grand...shockingly surprising...delightfully amazing...richly gratifying – I was reminded how little I truly understand of life. The most complex things I know pale – and that is not strong enough a word – in comparison to the movement of the universe.

I was reminded, whether I get it or not, God is in charge and while He plays at a totally different level...He is in the game!! I reminded of the scripture, "...what is man that thou art mindful of him..." and was grateful for His management style and the ride...

COFFEE AND CAMELS

> "To be content with what one has
> is the greatest and truest of riches…"
> - Cicero, On Duties

Her name was Botha, and her '…black as coal eyes…' were rich, liquid pools of mystery and stories yet untold. This was not the sort of thing one expects to find at six o'clock in the morning in a hotel in Dallas, Texas…and yet there we were!

The day before had been one of those unexpected '…classroom of life…' opportunities to get a measure as to whether I was getting a better handle on life.

I belong to a professional society that was having a site visit to Dallas for its national convention. I had been added to the team a little late in the process, and was looking forward to seeing some of the venues for the upcoming conference in the fall. In fact, the primary convention site and hotels had been chosen several years before….this visit was to choose between some places for smaller events around the edges of the meeting itself.

The team visited three facilities the evening of my arrival – it was great fun going behind the scenes of the Dallas Hard Rock Café and Mickey Gilley's famous honky-tonk western saloon and music hall. Both places had seen their share of the famous, the not so famous, and the '…über famous!' The site visit also provided time for personal interaction with the rest of the site visit team – a good thing.

One never knows...

Getting there had been a bit of an adventure. Traveling from the West Coast in the U.S. requires some planning, particularly when heading east. Because of the three hour difference, the airport is packed like sardines for the early morning flights...like the Grand Bazaar in Istanbul - people everywhere!

Whatever the airlines give you as an appropriate time to arrive at the airport, on those early morning flights heading east out of San Diego – seven days a week – getting there even earlier is a smart and wise thing to do. Then by eight or nine AM, the airport, relatively speaking, seems like a ghost town.

The flight would take three hours to Dallas, in the Central time zone, which was two hours later. Knowing I didn't need to be at the hotel until dinner, I headed out mid-morning – no problem...dinner was 5:30PM.

"No problem...", that is, until the flight was cancelled with no warning. The airline assured me it was not an issue; I would be sent out on the next flight. That was great, except the chess board had now been changed and the arrival window for dinner gone from a relaxed '...get there...clean up a little...feet up for a while...' to '...the dinner party will either be gathering to depart the hotel, or will already be gone by the time I arrive! '

The lesson? It didn't stir up a hornet's nest of anxiousness accompanying situations like this in my earlier years – a win!

All worked out well...I slid into the lobby of the hotel just as the group was gathering to leave. The team leader smiled and said, "Head up to your room. Do whatever you need to do. We can wait a few minutes." The evening was great fun and went well...all objectives accomplished. There would be a quick tour of the Dallas Convention Center in the morning, back to the airport and home.

Oh yeah, breakfast...

I had tucked in early after our evening out, got a great night's sleep and was ready for the day. There was a very small hitch in the morning…well there were two very small hitches. I'm a pretty early riser, and first thing in the morning put on the coffee pot to start my engines. I had drunk the room coffee the night before after returning from dinner – I know, it's a gift to be able to drink coffee at night and go straight to sleep. That would not be a problem because most hotels have early morning coffee…for some reason; this one didn't have coffee until 6am – no room coffee…no 'house coffee!'

Six it would be then!

At 5:50AM, I was waiting at the restaurant hoping someone would take a little compassion on me and let me get seated early…at least to get that coveted cup of coffee. 5:55AM – **enter Botha.**

"Would you like to sit down sir," she said with a lilt that gave her African origin away, but where? I'm not that good. "Yes I would," I replied with pleasant deliberateness. "Well, why don'cha sit right here in this booth. I'll bet you would like a cup of coffee." What a mind reader!

Botha was black as coal with matching eyes, and what appeared to be a little less than five feet (1.5 meters) in height. She looked to be in her mid-sixties, and had the sort of personality that begged the question…you know – how did she come to this country?

The Story…

She was Ethiopian and in her younger years had been a journalist under the Emperor Haile Selassie. In that time, she felt driven to write about the conditions in her country and found herself in jail where she was beaten and molested. After being let out, she continued to write.

Fortunately for her, she received warning the government was going to arrest her again. In the dark of night, leaving Ethiopia on a camel, crossing the Sudan; eventually she found herself in Algiers. From there it was France, Great Britain and finally here to the United States. What an adventure!!

I asked her how she liked living here, and she described how grateful she was to live in this country, and to have the life she was living. Life she was living? A mid-sixties woman working long hours for small wages and tips? Grateful for what? Poverty? Serving people who didn't even acknowledge her as a person,...whose wealth so exceeding her standard of living that even breakfast in the place she worked would be well beyond her financial bounds. Are you kidding me?

The reminders are important...

Ah yes, but a "...man's [woman's] life is more than the things that he [she] possesses..." Yes indeed. For Botha had something none of the money in the world could buy...gratitude for her life as it was...for the struggle...for the breath.

As we chatted in those brief moments, before the rush of the maddening crowd, we touched each other. I don't mean we shook hands or patted one another on the shoulder, I mean "...we touched each other..." and it was really good.

She said, "You are my first customer, and God brought you to me for a blessing at the start of my day."

I replied with a little more energy after that cup of coffee, "You are my first waitress, and there is little doubt God brought you to me for a blessing to start my day."

She grinned and leaned over closer quietly saying, "Thank you Jesus...we both been blessed."

Breakfast done...

I left that morning thinking about the scriptures and philosophers I had read...how they extoll the virtue of chasing life, not riches...how they admonish the emptiness of seeking pleasure...how they encourage the importance of finding one's place in life and performing their duty – not their profession – their duty as a human being.

I thought how Botha might share life's meaning with the hoards and hoards of us who believe that a little weight loss, a little extra money, a little more make up, or status might help us get over the hump of life. She hadn't read all those writers or tried all those things to find meaning. She just got up every morning with gratitude and did her job in the community of humanity.

I hopped on the glass-encased elevator, watching her as I headed up to my room on the 22nd floor and I couldn't help but smile as I heard her voice in that gentle lilt,

"Thank you Jesus..." and blessed we were!

WORDS CAN HURT, BUT...

> "...the words I speak unto you, they
> are spirit and they are life."
> - John 6:63, <u>Bible</u>

"Sticks and stones can break my bones, but words will never hurt me."

While my mother taught me more about the positive nature of life than any other person I have ever known, the above phrase was the one untruth she placed in my mind from the time I was a child.

There is little doubt she was simply passing along what she had been taught. A way to protect her child from what she knew life would bring to his mind. However, the defense was faulty...the intended 'barrier to entry' of hurts and tender feelings, left exposed...an unlocked backdoor into which ideas would pour, only to emerge at the most inopportune times in life.

In fact, 'words,' are truly the only things that can hurt 'us.'

What can we actually control?

Things that are not in our power are indifferent to 'us.' They are not really morally good or bad...the stoic philosophers would say things like health, wealth, poverty, disease, power and death...all of these things are external to us and act on us – they aren't moral issues...they are life. In spite of what we think, we have very few ways to influence these things beyond very minor adjustments.

Our thoughts and feelings, on the other hand...the words we

gather, the ideas we cultivate, the beliefs we keep within our minds – ah, now there is a different kettle of fish. It is here, and only here where we have real influence.

This, of course, is why self-help books are so popular. You can find the seven habits...the seven principles...the four dimensions...you know, the 'formula of the day' from which, with a little elbow grease and hard work, you can emerge as a meaningful and self-actuated human being!

It isn't just the ideas from the bookshelves full of these 'manuals for life' that fly into our notebooks...our personal libraries...our CD players...our iPods. All spiritual and philosophic writings point to peace and tranquility of the world in which we live – our minds. The Bible, Quran, Bhagavad Gita, Buddhist Dharma, Tao Te Ching...all of these texts extol the importance of internal stillness...the quieter one becomes, the more one hears...

We read stories of those who seem to have found 'it'...those who seem to have reached a state, or at least gotten close to some transcendent contentment. Even the founding documents of this country suggest we have the God given, and the independently declared, right to the "...pursuit of happiness?" Ah, the pursuit of happiness...the carrot before the donkey.

In fact, none of this internal satisfaction occurs without plain hard work. There are no '...road to Damascus...' experiences without having done a lot of preliminary preparation. The metaphoric story of the apple falling on Newton's head would have meant nothing without an enormous amount of mental preparation

Rubber meets the road...

You could read all of these texts, and indeed many are surely worth doing so. On the other hand, you could simply meet and hang around my friends, Paul and Monica...two of the most remarkable people I know. I'm not sure I would say that individually they are the two most remarkable people I know...although they surely are right up there. No, as a couple...a team...a partnership...a marriage – this is what makes them most remarkable.

Let me tell you what they know...better said, let me tell you what they understand about the importance of building internal worlds with each other. Their personal conversations during the day are littered with phrases like, "My darling husband you are so smart. What a great meal you have prepared." "You see how brilliant you are (Paul speaking to Monica), that was just the right solution!" The number of times "I love you" and "my darling" are repeated during the day are practically uncountable. The number of gentle touches and loving kisses immeasurable.

They do not live on another planet...nor in some alternate universe...they do not chant unintelligible mantras in saffron robes. They do understand the fragility of life, AND they understand the power of words – both loving and not so loving. They have made the conscious choice to edify, share, promote, and love one another in both word and deed! They have come to understand that incredible power comes from openness and vulnerability to one another. They have found the strength and will to live the words that these holy and spiritual writings profess.

This does not mean they do not have trials. As with all of us, they surely have, and if you knew them, you would understand those challenges have been significant. BUT – and Paul would not like me to use the word 'but' here, for he is an 'AND' person – BUT these two have made choices, hard working choices to promote one another's life journey...to constantly promote the love they feel for one another, AND the value that each brings to the other.

The lesson...
There is little doubt self examination and the seeking of contentment in life is the most important thing we can do. My friends Paul and Monica provide a living laboratory of what can be when people commit to promoting the life of another human being. They express in word, action, habit and character what is possible in the world of human interaction...both internally and externally through an unrelenting commitment to each other and the lives they live.

Quoting the philosopher Lao Tzu:

"Watch your thoughts; they become words.
Watch your words; they become actions.
Watch your actions; they become habits.
Watch your habits; they become character.
Watch your character; it becomes your destiny."

Accomplish this, and in fact, words will never hurt you.

SOMEONE WAS AT THE DOOR

One should seek wisdom...
better yet – understanding
Proverbs 4:7, <u>Bible</u>

The sign on the front door said, "NO SOLICITATION"

The knocking persisted anyway. As I headed to the living room to see who was there, I wondered whether the person might be unable to read the English – I would need to fix that.

There they were...a woman and a young girl – a diminutive eight (8) year old in a plain dress and shoulder length light brown hair.

"I'm sorry, we take no solicitations." The woman, yet unnamed, replied, "Well, we are not selling anything. We just wanted to give you this."

And with that, she held out a nicely printed religious tract suggesting I might find answers to some deeper truths.

Another day, another time...
As I looked at the Jehovah's Witness marketing piece, I was immediately taken back to a small trailer outside of Fort Rucker, Alabama where I spent the last year in military service. It was the fall of 1970 and the 'Witnesses' were preparing for the end of the world in 1975. The young man had been coming to my trailer for a couple of weeks, but on this particular day brought one of the elders to answer the questions he knew would 'seal the deal' for his proselyte

quota. The impending 'world's end' had fed the intensity of their work.

In the early 70s, 'Witnesses' numbers were growing and their efforts (always impressive) were at full steam. It wasn't, of course, the first time. Their leadership unsuccessfully forecast the coming of Christ in 1874...then later 1914 followed by some of the prophets in 1925. There had been other bold prophetic expressions over the years...too numerous to list here – background noise...all background noise.

Who are these people?

These gentle folk are often treated rudely, and with discomfort by people on the receiving end of 'cold calls.' On the other hand, friendliness, curiosity and courtesy toward them are often mistakenly interpreted as potential 'fish for the net' of the Kingdom – their Kingdom, of course.

I looked at the brochure and chatted a little with, ah...well, I needed to ask.

"I'm sorry for being impolite, what are your names? My name is Ted."

"Karen and my daughter is Harper," she replied.

"Harper?" I said to the young girl. "Why, that is an interesting name. Have you heard of Harper Lee, the author of 'To Kill a Mockingbird'?"

If Harper's smile could have gotten any wider, it would have swallowed up the day!

"I was named for her, and mom has a signed copy of the book she is going to give to me when I am older."

I squatted down so Harper and I could see each other eye to eye. I told her I was impressed that she was brave to come with her mother this day, and I encouraged her faith. I gave her, a familiar (at least to me) child version of making sure she studied hard in school. I said I was confidant God had a plan for her life and only she would know what that was.

There are few things in life I enjoy more than connecting with children…yes sir, I hit a home run with Harper!

We had a pleasant conversation – the three of us. I posed a question or two that gave Karen pause. Questions are often a great way to help people sort through their belief structure. She had no way of knowing I was well versed in the 'Witness' history and doctrine from years of study in a small religious community.

Karen, not able to answer the questions, indicated she would be back with the answers. Maybe so…maybe not…it seldom actually happens, but if there were a next time it would NOT be in the company of Harper. I had my chance with Ms. Harper and it was, as it usually is with children, lovely!

Back to Karen…
So here were Karen and Harper standing at my door, exercising their faith…acting on their belief…trying, of course, to convince me of a particular teaching, that for them, regardless of what others believed, had brought order and consistency to their lives.

Certainly, one could argue doctrine and ideology, but really what is the purpose of the scripture? Christ only 'fought' against hypocrisy and evil in religious leaders. The common folk? He loved them…fed them…provided parables for them…taught them through example after example. Asked them a question or two they couldn't answer that might get them thinking.

There is no context in the New Testament for using the scripture to strike a blow to the seeking heart. There is no context in the New Testament to feel superior because of a particular faith. There is no context in the New Testament for a specific… particular…unique…special teaching that, in the Christian context, betters all others.

On the front steps of my home this week, Karen, Harper and I found that place of respect and humanity. It was lively, respectful and it was "...very good."

KIDS...YOU'VE GOT TO LOVE THEM

> "If children are our future, connecting with them in
> the present increases our vision of the future,
> and brings meaning to our past..."
> - anonymous

I've enjoyed children pretty much all of my life. I mean, I liked 'em when I was one of them, maybe because I felt like I belonged...you know, a group of little people that seemed like me! As I grew older with that group – those youngsters who became my contemporaries, I never lost my connection with the 'little people'...

When I'm around them, it's invigorating. Some high-end psychotherapist might suggest a diagnosis like 'Peter Pan Syndrome,' or some other more serious sounding, and completely unpronounceable name...but for me? I just like kids.

Over the years, I have learned to communicate with them. It's odd to say I have 'learned' to communicate, I mean, we are the same species after all...

Somehow, however, while we are in the business of learning our alphabet, how to use numbers, and the way to act in a socially acceptable way, our child-speak seems to slip away. Of course, maturing and become a self-actualized adult has value, but it does come at a cost.

Here are a few things I have learned. Before I reveal things that work for me, let me be clear...my wife and I have not had children.

This is important, because I have missed that middle of the night colic; flues, chickenpox, bumps, scratches and myriad of other events that might cause one to be grateful the early child years are done.

Also, these techniques are not particularly valuable before children can walk or talk. When they are babies, they don't discriminate much and seem to react to simple cooing, gently single syllable words, loving, non-threatening smiles, and for reasons unknown to me, higher pitched voices. Even the biggest of manly men, somehow seem to automatically raise the pitch, and soften the edge, of their voices when speaking to them.

Note: this may be directed more toward men, because women... well, women seem to be inherently wired for this sort of thing.

Things that work for me…

Now that we have set the criterion, here is my recipe…the few things that almost always work:

- Do everything you can to become their size.
  - o Crouch down (or sit down) so that you can look them in the eye…or as much in the eye as possible.
  - o When you are a child, adults are huge. Communicating with them can be intimidating from the point of view of…well, the point of view of – up!!
  - o Forgotten what it's like? Crank your neck back and look up at the ceiling for five minutes or so…you will immediately resonate with what I am saying.
  - o For someone like me, who for most of his adult life has been 6'5" (1.98m), picking a child of at least 3 feet (.9m) in height is a bit easier…on their necks and my knees.
- Keep a distance of three to four feet (.9-1.2m0. There are good reasons for this:
  - o Usually the child slips behind their Mum or Dad's legs. Providing space keeps them from feeling crowded, AND their parents from feeling you are interested in their (parent's) knees!
  - o Secondarily, it is good if the child can see all of you

at once as you are crouched...they will naturally look for your eyes.

   o Thirdly, it is much easier to look at you if you are lower to the ground rather than the size of a small skyscraper.

- Keep your hands within the width and height of your shoulders, and do not...I repeat...DO NOT reach out for the child.

- Smile; say little complimentary things, whilst looking them gently in the eye.

- Eyes are the windows to the soul. Your face may be smiling, but the sincerity of your eyes will tell the story every time.

The objective here is to get the child to move out just a little from the safety of its parent's legs. This often happens slowly...maybe not at all, but when it does, it is not a bad idea to move back just a little giving the child a little more space.

Once the youngster feels safe, he or she will begin to open up which is what you were after from the start. SUCCESS!!

Forewarned is forearmed...
Now a word of caution...Opening the child's 'trust and confidence' box can be a two-edged sword. It should NEVER be done for the sake of trying to impress the parents or others. I say this, because once that child trusts you, you need to be absolutely prepared for what happens next.

For some children, it is just a gentle smile and a few words and gestures, out in the open, as it were...a nice, enjoyable and meaningful interchange.

On the other hand, if the child has a lot of unpredictable, un-stored energy, you must be prepared to receive whatever the little one expresses. You may find yourself perceived as a new playmate...you may become the center of their attention as long as you are in the general vicinity.

The payoff...

There are few things in life...at least in my life...that are as rewarding as capturing the attention of a child long enough to return to the unbridled joy and life of my childhood. It is refreshing, feeding and brings with it the reward of reconnecting to the universe in a meaningful way.

When I have the opportunity to practice this skill, I hardly ever turn it down, because it almost never...almost never disappoints.

If you find yourself consumed with the day-to-day grind, and focused on the 'important matters of life,' try the experiment. Next time you are in proximity and have the opportunity...the children, grandchildren, dare I say great grandchildren of your friends...even your own — try the formula, or parts of it, out.

Trust me on this, there is little in life that is as refreshing as engaging a mind that has not been yet burdened with the matters of life...the experience will unburden yours!!

MENU PLEASE

*"Nothing would be more tiresome than eating
and drinking if God had not made them
a pleasure as well as a necessity..."*
- Voltaire

I have a young friend finding herself at a decision-making place in her life. Actually, I suppose, I don't know anybody who isn't. Isn't everything about making decisions, really? I suppose it's just a matter of magnitude.

At any rate, it's a professional choice. There are a number of options in front of her and she is not completely clear what she should do. It isn't a decision between right and wrong – that would be a much longer topic! While the decision is important, it's more like looking at the menu and trying to decide between the Lamb and the Beef or if.

What to do...
We spend a lot of our lives trying to figure out what it is we are supposed to do with the 'big picture' self. I suspect for a lot of us, we actually never find out. We just sort of show up, and with the most modest of forethought, do whatever appears in front of us. I mean, how do we really know?

I should say in the first instance that I believe in God, AND I believe that He has a plan for each of us...as a part of something bigger. The apostle Paul says each of us has a gift, likening it to a body part with each gift working together making the 'entire body' (mankind) function as it was intended. In other words, find our calling and work our lives in it. Finding that calling is the result of a lot of little decisions we make.

Thinking God has a specific plan for us, however, could be seen to be a level of hubris with a capital 'H'…maybe even a capital 'S!' It does seem a little arrogant to believe the Creator of the universe…the Author of intelligent design…the Originator of the 'tertium quid' (sometimes described as: beyond chance and necessity…you know the spiritual side of things), would take the time to consider us as individuals?

I know, for many of us, it is simply a matter of faith…a matter of acceptance. BUT is it that simple? Don't we have some part in it? We are 'free moral agents' aren't we? There is consequence to choice isn't there? I mean, don't we at least need to look at the menu?

"Faith without works is dead…"

Believing God has a plan for us, and actually finding out what that plan is, are probably two completely different things. "Finding our place…" is not just a matter of faith, it is a matter of choice…and choice is a matter of action. After all the scripture does say, "Ask and you shall receive, seek and you will find, knock and the door will be opened for you…" Ask, seek and knock are all action verbs…we need to do something!

Do something…ah yes, find something to do…when all else fails, do something! There is a reason these action verbs are part of the center-piece of our faith, for without asking, seeking, knocking, nothing happens. When nothing happens things remain the same. When everything remains the same…well, you know, they stop growing. When things stop growing they lose relevance. When things lose relevance, they die…

I'm not clear whether my young friend will choose the "…Lamb" or "…Beef," but I know she will make a choice. That choice will lead to others and as long as she continues to ask the questions, seek for the answers, and knock on the doors of the unknown, she will continue to grow.

Pardonnez-moi, que aimez-<u>vous</u> pour le dîner ? – Pardon me, what would <u>you</u> like for dinner?

GRAVITY, NOT JUST A GOOD IDEA...IT'S THE LAW

> "You can break the law and pay the price,
> but bending it is not an option."
> - Anonymous

"Gravity is not just a good idea, it's the law!"

A fellow, named Gerry Mooney coined this phrase in 1977, while in Tulsa Oklahoma during the American gas crisis. He saw an ad campaign on television that said, "The 55 mph speed limit. It isn't a good idea. It's the law!" It inspired him to change the words "…speed limit…" to gravity. His gravity phrase has now appeared in an uncountable number of places, mostly attributed to "… - anonymous…"

This phrase got me to thinking about other things. For example:

- Heartbeats are not a good idea, they are the law
- Breathing is not a good idea, it is the law
- Digestion is not a good idea, it is the law

These are examples of what philosophers call 'natural law' which some say is the 'order of the universe.' They describe the unavoidable "…what is…" in opposition to the "…nice if it were…"

Many things in our daily lives come under the natural law such as the air we breathe, the water we drink, the food we produce, but we take them for granted, because they...well, because they simply are part of the universal order to which we unconsciously adhere. It is only when we find ourselves at the edges of the law we notice its reality, for example when we fall (gravity) or when our health fails in some way (i.e. heart, breathing or digestive problems).

I've been thinking about another part of the natural law, and that is the event toward which we began traveling the day of our birth...the unavoidable end of our lives. I've been thinking about how so many of us fear the loss of life, because we perceive it as theft of what we have and know, and because we have no idea what lies beyond, if anything at all. While death is as much a part of the natural law as gravity...the beating of our heart...the breaths we take...the digestion that helps nutrient absorption...it seems to fall into a different category in our thought process.

Why is it we view death differently than other parts of the law we readily and almost unconsciously accept? Why is it that we embrace, "From dust thou art..." and resist "...to dust thou shalt return...?"

At birth we knew nothing, and consequently did not fear the unknown...we just slipped to the planet's surface and began the expedition. Why should we not simply embrace death as part of the process and celebrate its approach as much as anything else along the way? After all, it is a pretty big event in our lives. The argument could be made that it is as exciting (if I might use that word) a marker as the entrance we made at birth! I mean, at birth all was unknown and the tablet was blank. At death, no matter the length of our lives, the diary has stuff written all over it!

I've been thinking about this for a couple of reasons.

The first is that this week marks the death of my younger sister Nancy. It was February 12th, 2012 when breath left her. We were there at the end, and as is the parting ways with someone you love, the experience was both painful and exquisite – painful because this soul with whom we had shared so much slipped from our grasp as a dream dissolves with the coming of a new day...exquisite because being with her in life and sharing her last moments, provided a kind of closure I had not expected. Her birth represented only a diversion of attention from me to her in our household. Her death carried for me the experience of being in the complete life cycle of another human being. An experience I have had with no other…and will probably never have again.

The other reason is that my last breath is approaching, in small, yet clearly discernable increments. In the early, middle and even these latter years, I didn't think much about my own death. I should hasten to add, I do not give it an undue amount of thought, but I have drawn some deliberate conclusions about its impending appearance in my life.

"…in my life…" an odd way to express the end, but then again the ending of the cycle is as natural (natural law) as everything experienced from the first gasp of air in to the last expression of air out. It is all about the 'cycle,' and that brings me to why I do not fear death, but in the most fascinating (to me) of ways look forward, with a kind of curiosity, to its arrival.

It is simply that cycles are just that…they end only to begin again…breathe in, breathe out – the small breaths that keep us alive moment to moment – each breath out a kind of death, as each breath in represents the next moment of life.

I have no doubt in the BIG cycle of BREATH (breath in at birth…breath out at death) is also just that…a cycle from which the next life experience is renewed. I have no doubt my sister's BIG BREATH was a cycle from which she emerged into the next cycle, and I have no doubt it will be that way for me…hence the curiosity, not fear with which I look forward to the application of the natural law in my life.

It is not just that I accept by faith the 'hope' instilled in me that there is a better place after this life. It is not just because I have been told that in my "…Father's house are many mansions…"

I embrace this, because you see, the cycle of life…the 'CYCLE' of life is not just a good idea…it is the law!

IT'S IN THE REARVIEW MIRROR

"A cat, even when mortally ill, keeps those wide calm
eyes focused on the ever-changing kaleidoscope
of the here-and-now. There is no thought
of death, and hence no fear of it."
- Lanza R, Berman B. Biocentrism

It was close…so close that everything around us felt as though it were standing still. There was quiet chatting, but the sounds seemed, in that moment, to completely disappear. One might say it was surreal…

The time had was at hand…
As the hardwood trees of the north present brilliantly colored leaves in the death throes of their short lives, so the season of my sister's life had come to an end. We had all been drawn to this place, not simply because it *was* the end, but rather by some primal urge to be part of the transition…a powerful and compelling feeling that there was *nothing else* we could do…*nowhere else* we could be. In the oddest of ways, it was quietly comforting to be in this place to say good-bye.

Saying good-bye…this was not a "…see you later…" or "…see you in the morning…" This was not a "…see you…" at all. It was standing on the wharf of life watching a loved one walk up the gangplank with a one-way ticket in hand…. it *was* the end.

There would be no more tomorrows…no quick and knowing glances that come only from the intimacy of the years…no inside jokes that comfort one in their familiarity. No indeed, the end was coming with the unrelenting mass of a one hundred car freight train entering the darkest of tunnels…too much momentum…there would be no turning back.

Some things can't be explained…

In those final moments, fixed securely in my mind, I took her drawn and shrunken face in my hands. I leaned in to whisper how deeply I loved her – her skin cool and surprisingly soft. In the most primitive of ways, I rubbed her cheek with my cheek…her forehead with my forehead…her neck with mine. It was as though I hoped I could give her heat and life where there was no heat and little life.

Her daughter Mariah had been putting lotion on her face and dehydrated lips…some saline drops on her closed and dry eyelids. As the tide was slipping quickly away, I was compelled, to open her eyes and gaze one last time…to see if there were something I could understand…some comfort in this comfortless moment.

During the final months of her life, the brightness of her eyes, those sparkling windows of the soul had begun to dim like the greying waters of a stagnant pond robbed of its underground spring. They had slowly taken on a dullness that added injury to the insult of watching her life drift away into the darkness of a starless winter's sky.

In that most intimate of moments, something magical happened. Magic…there is no magic…for magic is but illusion. Yet in that moment, as I opened her eyes, I was captured by their liquid clarity. I am not sure I have ever looked into the eyes of another human being that were so clear. Those eyes…those eyes transcended the devastating disease that had stolen my sister's life like a thief in the night. Something happened that moment for which I simply do not have the words to express…no well so deep, no ocean so wide, no universe so expansive that can speak to that moment.

Nancy and I had always been close…the closeness that comes from years together, tempered by the knowledge that we liked each other…we loved each other…in many ways celebrated each other.

160

Love simply is...

Love is one of those curiosities of the human condition. Writers, who in their self-indulgent wisdom separate love into different categories, often amuse me. I get there is a difference between affection and carnal love, but all of it...all of it finds itself on the continuum of an expression reduced to this: Whatever the motive, love is the long distance run of unfettered affection...the volume of which can be as high as the loudest audio speakers at a rock concert and as subtle and soft as the brush of silk against a young child's cheek. No matter the 'volume' there is a texture of unbreakable strength in the desire to know and be known. "For God so loved the world..."

In those last moments, lost in the clarity of my sister's translucent eyes, there was a conversation...a dialogue...an indescribable knowing. It was clear there was no fear, no sense of discomfort regarding the unknown. There was an understanding...a softness...a comfort and consolation...for me! Her final gift.

Five minutes later she was gone...she had slipped away...the ship freed of its mooring moved beyond the horizon.

Retro – no *intro*spection...

I am not sure I have ever experienced a moment with any living creature as intimate as those, and yet even now I cannot recapture their richness. Writing these words has been an attempt to record them...revisit them...relive them if possible, but of course it is not possible. The scripture says that after the Angel visited Mary to tell her of the impending birth of the Christ, she "...pondered these things in her heart..."

As I "ponder" the last moments of my sister's life, in my heart, I find the edges are softer...less clear...not so focused nor intense. BUT this I do know, the brown liquid windows to her soul spoke to mine...touched me...expressing in those wordless moments the ancient expression..."Let not your heart be troubled, neither let it be afraid..."

I long to touch that soul once again...I have little doubt I will...

Made in the USA
Middletown, DE
13 August 2015